Case Material and Role Play in Counselling Training

JANET TOLAN AND SUSAN LENDRUM

London and New York

First published 1995
by Routledge
11 New Fetter Lane, London EC4P 4EE

Simultaneously published in the USA and Canada
by Routledge
29 West 35th Street, New York, NY 10001

© 1995 Janet Tolan and Susan Lendrum

Typeset in Garamond by Solidus (Bristol) Limited

Printed and bound in Great Britain by
Clays Ltd, St. Ives PLC

British Library Cataloguing in Publication Data
A catalogue record for this book is available from the British Library

Library of Congress Cataloguing in Publication Data
A catalogue record for this book has been requested.

ISBN 0-415-10214-6 (hbk)
ISBN 0-415-10215-4 (pbk)

CONTENTS

Acknowledgements   vii

PART I USING THE MATERIALS

Introduction   3

**1 Why Use Case Materials and Role Play in Counselling
    Training?**   6
   Rationale   6
   The importance of empathy   7
   The importance of trainee self-awareness   9
   The importance of course members' responsibility for learning   10
   The importance of the trainer–course member relationship   12
   The importance of equal opportunities   13
   The elements within a training course   13
   Conclusion   17

2 Case Material: Purposes and Procedure   19
   Purposes of case material   19
   Uses of case material in developing empathy   20
   Procedure for case material   22

3 Basic Role Play: Purpose and Procedure   26
   Purpose of role play   26
   Projected and personal role play: participant roles   27
   Procedure for basic personal role play   31
   Development of personal role play as training progresses   36
   Procedure for basic projected role play   36
   Tutor observation   39

4 Role Play Variations   40
   Purpose of varying role play methods   40
   Horseshoe   41
   Excuse me   45
   Rondelle   45

v

Demonstration fishbowl   46
Group and linked role plays   47
Variations on the variations   52
Conclusion   54

5   Adapting Case and Role Play Materials   55
Introduction   55
Levels of training   55
Use of key questions for different objectives   58
Altering the complexity of the material   62
Adapting for different work contexts   66
Equal opportunities or difference and discrimination   70
Conclusion   71

PART II THE RESOURCES

How to use Part II   75

Materials Reference Table   80
Section A   Core Relationship Skills   80
Section B   Practice Themes   81
Categories across sections A and B   82

Section A   Core Relationship Skills Material   83
A1   Core conditions: the basis for trust   83
A2   Developing the relationship   95
A3   Beginnings and endings   103
A4   Ethics and good practice   118

Section B   Practice Themes Material   141
B1   Loss (general)   142
B2   Bereavement   148
B3   Change and transition   159
B4   Sexuality   163
B5   Race and culture   169
B6   Disability   171
B7   Stress, anxiety, depression   173

APPENDIXES

Appendix 1: Categorisation of the Forms of Resource Material   181
Appendix 2: Examples of Case Material Handouts   185

Index   190

ACKNOWLEDGEMENTS

Thanks to all the many trainers and course members who have worked with us over the years. Their energy and ideas are present in this book. Particular thanks to Pauline Quinn, Anne Lord and Gabrielle Syme, who have allowed us to use some of their materials; and to our daughters, Ruth, who slaved over a hot word processor, and Vanessa, who supplied coffee and truffles.

PART I
Using the materials

INTRODUCTION

ABOUT THE METHODS

The value of case material and role play lies in their capacity to stimulate the imagination and enable course members to engage with people's concerns and complexities within the supportive environment of the course. In this way, course members are able to develop the understanding and skills of counselling and prepare themselves to work effectively with their future clients.

There are many challenges for course members in experiential work. If they are used to a more cognitive way of working, they may feel very uncertain and vulnerable about having the spotlight upon their feelings and behaviour. Role play highlights the differences between how people *think* they are communicating and how their communication is perceived by others, and when course members recognise the potential for learning in this method they begin to demand more.

Case study and role play methods can be as exciting and challenging for the trainer as for the learner. They often evoke the unexpected, since course members use their own experiences and imagination in working with them. As tutors, we need to draw fully upon our own skills and understanding to make this wealth of material useful to a training group.

Unlike many other areas of education and training, relationship work is centrally concerned with ourselves. We are not dealing with tools or machines, with manipulating figures or words on the page. There is nothing to provide distance, either between course members and their clients or between tutors and course members. The developments which people seek from counselling arise from the relationship between counsellor and client. Similarly, the development of course members arises in large part from the relationship between themselves and course tutors. Quite frankly, this level of engagement can be exhausting. We have worked with course members who, at different stages, revere us, batter us, love us, hate us, are frightened of us, are angry with us, support us, challenge us. It is the most stimulating, frustrating, rewarding work we know.

As trainers, our purpose is not to develop 'nice' people, 'mature' people or 'more rounded' people (although this might be one outcome of the training), but to develop practitioners – people who can use their insights, awareness and perceptions in a skilled way to benefit others. This is why experiential teaching/learning methods are essential and why we have chosen to focus on case material and role play in this book.

Using these methods, however, is considerably less 'safe' than using more didactic methods. Course tutors are most effective when they model those skills and attributes which they are advocating for course members. It is important for us to demonstrate empathy, congruence and unconditional positive regard; to support and challenge course members and each other. We cannot hide behind theory or misuse the power we have as tutors to cover our own vulnerabilities – however tempting this may be at times. We have learned that course members are more than willing to forgive us our mistakes – and learn from them – if we acknowledge them openly. For example, 'Perhaps I expressed that clumsily. I'm sorry. How could I have said it better?'

We have found that there are many temptations for us as trainers. Being a guru, for example: it can be *so* seductive to have course members at our (metaphorical) feet, telling us how wonderful we are and how they will never be able to do it like that – so much for empowerment!

Wanting to be loved is another: it is tempting not to challenge course members, for when we do so, however respectfully, they can get cross, or feel aggrieved, or get upset, or even leave the course. As if this were not risky enough of itself, other course members can get protective of their peers and start accusing us too.

Being the fount of all wisdom is a third temptation; hiding behind a convenient bit of jargon is, after all, much less scary than admitting we don't know. And it is also tempting to blame the slowness or resistance of course members rather than face discomfort in ourselves.

So how do we avoid these and other such traps? A co-tutor who will support us and our course members when we risk being real and open – and challenge us when we don't – will help us not to fall into the traps in the first place. And a training supervisor who will help us first to recognise the traps we are in and, second, to find our way out, is also beyond price.

ABOUT OURSELVES

We first met when we were both asked to develop a validation scheme for counselling training in the North-West and, once the scheme was in operation, to put on a 'Training for Trainers' course. In planning for this course, we discovered that each of us found role play and case materials extraordinarily effective in all kinds of relationship training, whether for voluntary bereavement counsellors, psychotherapists, people managers or counselling supervisors. We also discovered that we had developed our own materials and ways of using them and realised that no text existed which detailed this kind of experience. Neither, as far as we are aware, is there a book which offers material which can be used across the full range of training.

ABOUT THE BOOK

This book is intended, first, to help beginning trainers to use case studies and role plays in their work; second, to help experienced trainers to expand their repertoire of training methods; and third, and perhaps most importantly, to provide a range of material which can be used and adapted for relationship training at all levels.

Part I of this book covers the rationale and general principles of using case discussion and role play methods and gives detailed notes on how to use them in training programmes and how to adapt them to different contexts and levels. Part II contains over 250 case and role play materials, structured for easy access, together with practical tips for trainers.

Case study and role play methods are appropriate to a wide range of training activities: listening and interpersonal skills training; counselling skills training; counselling and psychotherapy training. To avoid repetition we often use the term 'relationship training' to cover all of these. Similarly, the terms for the two main roles, 'counsellor' and 'client' are used over a wide range of practice. We expect that readers will change the terms, using 'listener' or 'therapist', say, if more appropriate to their own training group.

Throughout this book we have decided to use the personal pronouns 'he' for course members and 'she' for trainers, rather than the cumbersome 'she or he' or an ungrammatical 'they'.

ABOUT YOU

Whatever your involvement in training, we hope that you will find this book stimulating and useful.

1

WHY USE CASE MATERIALS AND ROLE PLAY IN COUNSELLING TRAINING?

RATIONALE

Give sorrow words: the grief that does not speak
Whispers the oe'r-fraught heart, and bids it break.
Macbeth, IV, iii

These words of Shakespeare are often quoted in the context of counselling because they so aptly express, even today, the value of putting deepest feelings into words, especially when those words can be heard and accepted by another person. Shakespeare also warns of the unhappy consequences, such as the sense of a broken heart, when feelings are not openly expressed. We could describe Macduff's situation as follows:

Macduff is a Scottish Lord whose castle has been attacked in his absence and his wife and young children slaughtered by the agents of a certain Macbeth who fears being replaced one day by Macduff's son. Macduff is a man of action who could easily respond without being fully aware of the feelings which motivate him. He might rush out to tackle Macbeth without forethought, thus putting his and others' lives in danger. His old friend Malcolm knows how important it is for him to put his shock, pain and sorrow into words.

Or as a latter-day case vignette as follows:

Mr Macduff is a wealthy man whose wife and children have just been killed in a road traffic accident where a drunken driver crossed the central reservation and ploughed into the oncoming traffic. Macduff is a man of action who could easily respond without being fully aware of the feelings which motivate him. He might rush out to the scene of the accident, or to find the drunken driver, without forethought, thus putting his and others' lives in danger. His old friend Malcolm knows how important it is for him to put his shock, pain and sorrow into words.

Further, we could let readers enter more intensely into the feelings of this experience through offering two role plays as follows:

Mr Macduff

You are a 35-year-old man whose wife and children have just been killed in a horrific road traffic accident. You cannot believe that anyone could be that drunkenly crazy or that this could have happened to you ...

Mr Malcolm

You were with your old friend Macduff when his brother-in-law Ross arrived to tell him that his wife and children had just been killed in an accident. You know that Macduff could easily rush out into action rather than expressing his feelings more directly. You know that it is important for him to put his shock, pain and sorrow into words ...

How can counsellors learn to respond appropriately to Macduff? And how can we, as trainers, help counsellors to respond to Macduff? As counsellors, we face the simple but difficult task of being respectful, congruent and empathic towards Macduff. As trainers, we face the double task of being respectful, congruent and empathic to the trainee counsellor, while also ensuring that he or she learns most effectively how to be with and respond to Macduff.

By first of all considering Macduff's tragedy as a case vignette and then by entering it more intensely as a role play, we can be more in touch with what is really happening for Macduff and we are in a more powerful position to practise responding to him in words.

Counsellors need to learn how to enable others to put their feelings into words. We, as trainers, need to find ways of helping counsellors to enter the feeling world of another and to respond appropriately to that other. These familiar lines from Macbeth can perhaps highlight the value of case studies and role plays. Courses would usually start with less dramatic materials. Nevertheless there remains the twofold training task of enabling learners: (i) to enter into the feeling world of another person *and* (ii) to practise responding to that person in distress, in other words, to respond empathically.

THE IMPORTANCE OF EMPATHY

The development of empathic responding is fundamental to both the theory and practice of relationship training. Empathy involves, first, perceiving the feeling experience of another person and, second, communicating to that person an understanding of the experience. In order to arrive at the point where they are able to begin empathising with others, course members must tackle several strands of learning at the same time, each strand interwoven with and complementing the others.

The first strand is that of becoming *aware* of their own feelings. We live in a society which tends to value the cognitive, rational and intellectual more highly than the affective, feeling and emotional. In fact, 'Don't get emotional about it' is often a severe reproof, particularly if directed at a man. 'Emotional' in this sense often has undertones of childishness and loss of control. It is not surprising, then, that many people believe that their own feelings and emotions are, at best, a weakness and, at worst, shameful. They have learned to repress, distort or ignore them. As awareness of their own feelings is low, so, too is awareness of others' feelings.

The second strand of learning is for trainees to re-tune to the signals which indicate emotions *in others*; posture, facial expression and tone of voice, as well as the words spoken.

A third strand is learning to *accept* their own and others' feelings – to discover that there are no 'good' or 'bad' feelings, only natural responses which can be understood if the context is known (and, moreover, that repression and distortion can be understood in context).

A fourth strand is developing a vocabulary with which to *communicate* feelings and emotions, particularly the nuances. Perhaps it would be more accurate to say vocabular*ies* since, for example, those working with teenagers may need significantly different sets of words from those working with retired people.

The fifth and last strand involves course members in *separating* their own feelings from those of others. When they hear something with which they identify, they will learn not to rush in with identifying statements assuming the other person's experience and responses to be identical to their own. This brings us back to strand one, for if course members deny their own individual feelings in relation to a particular situation or experience, they will fail to recognise the separateness of others' feelings, and will not be able to open themselves to the feeling world of the other.

Course members move along all these strands simultaneously, each one complementing and reinforcing the other. Examples of this are common: the person who hears another's feelings named recognises his own; the person who receives acceptance of her feelings can herself begin to accept them; the person who hears another's response to a situation understands that his is not the only possible response. Most of all, the whole learning group recognises that the feelings and emotions which they have guarded and kept private are shared by many others. Understandably, this is a process which intensifies as the course progresses, and is a process which often needs much practice if really useful levels of empathy are to be achieved.

THE IMPORTANCE OF TRAINEE SELF-AWARENESS

Case materials and role plays are potentially powerful vehicles for accessing the affective world. As a course member becomes more aware of his affective world, his confidence in that world grows and he becomes more aware of the value of his own inner world and of his own 'self'. He discovers that the nature and uniqueness of his own life experience can actually contribute to his affective learning. He discovers too that his growing self-awareness is an essential prerequisite for the growth of empathy towards others. And as he increasingly recognises and values his own feelings and experience, so he becomes more able to recognise and value these in others.

On occasions, a course member will find himself experiencing strong feelings of which he was unaware and which have been 'triggered' by the case study or role play. When case materials trigger such feelings in course members they may well experience high levels of anxiety and may react by projecting some of the uncomfortable, but often unrecognised, feelings on to other course members or on to the tutors themselves. In the early stages of training, an individual may feel quite overwhelmed by such feelings and other members of the group, who themselves are probably experiencing strong feelings, may also struggle to respond appropriately to the projections. Trainers need to manage these projections right from the start and to recognise that angry reactions may be covering needy or painful feelings at the edge of awareness. It is important that the trainers model good counselling practice in responding to such occurrences, respecting and acknowledging the feelings, both overt and covert, of the individual and the other group members.

It is more appropriate for trainers to work with the feelings evoked within the group – embarrassment, vulnerability, helplessness, neediness and so on – than with the original personal material triggered in the individual. It is an important aspect of relationship training for the whole group to recognise that if they are to be able to help clients with aspects of their emotional worlds then course members themselves will first have to have worked through relevant areas of their own unresolved material. This might be through group work on the course or through their own counselling therapy.

It is important for trainers to communicate clearly and confidently that all relationship training involves this kind of personal development, since course members in the early stages of training are often frightened of the feelings which begin to emerge. Self-awareness is as important, of course, for trainers as it is for counsellors. Our own confidence and competence in the feeling world will be enhanced through experiences of therapy. Holding the boundary between training and personal therapy on the course is just one of the trainer functions for which awareness on the part of the trainer is necessary to good practice and good modelling.

It is particularly important for the course to have clear and openly acknowledged structures which can function to contain any anxieties evoked by the training. Course publicity should make it clear that participants will be expected to use their own experiences as a basis for learning in order to achieve objectives which involve affective development, since there is nothing which increases resistance so much as participants' sense that the rules were hidden from them until after they had agreed to play the game.

THE IMPORTANCE OF COURSE MEMBERS' RESPONSIBILITY FOR LEARNING

When giving any information or outline of relationship training, it is important to strike the balance between offering enough information so that potential participants and their managers know what they are 'buying into', while still offering course members the possibility of taking some ownership of the course. One way of doing this is to be clear about the course *objectives* – the outcomes which they can expect – while reserving the possibility of tailoring the *content* and *methods* to the needs of a particular group. Take, for example, the following objective, that:

> By the end of the course, participants should, in their everyday work,
> be able to paraphrase, reflect feelings and summarise.

Tutors may discover that participants are working with large numbers of elderly people and may decide to bring in material on this age group, such as stereotypes about older people, to raise awareness in the course membership of older people's real concerns and how to respond to them. In this instance, although the objectives remain the same, the *content* is determined by course members' learning need to hear and respond to their older clients.

Another example in relation to the same objective would be if course members express a preference for using a particular *method*, say video recording or horseshoe role play, to develop skills; then, provided that difficulties are not being unnecessarily avoided and that the agreed objective is achieved, the tutor can be flexible about the learning methods.

Flexibility does, however, have its limitations and it is important to remain firm about, for instance, the stated objectives (and experiential methods of achieving them) or the confidentiality rules or ethical issues associated with training. Because trainers are expecting participants to work at a very personal level in developing relationship skills, they often have to consider ethical issues. The British Association for Counselling has produced a *Code of Ethics and Practice for Trainers* which is very helpful in highlighting potential difficulties and giving guidance.

The course objectives are one of the basic elements of the contract between a course provider and the individual or organisational client or clients. However much or little scope there is for participant choice in curriculum and method (and there may be relatively little choice in these areas for short courses, particularly with heterogeneous groups), it is always important to set up a framework for continuous self-evaluation. From the very beginning it is useful to use self-evaluation exercises and then move on to exercises which include course members seeking regular feedback from peers and tutors about their developing skills. This in turn helps to create a climate and a context within which self-evaluation and other evaluative skills are highly valued and prized.

Thus course members learn to evaluate the development of their counselling skills through the media of case studies and role plays. Such a sense of responsibility for their own learning is, perhaps, the single most important factor in enabling course members to achieve the course objectives.

Just as all helping relationships are fundamentally about empowerment of clients, so all relationship training which practises what it preaches is about empowerment of course members. This may run counter to many course members' expectations and to those of their employing authorities and institutions. Part of the initial difficulty for those unused to this way of working may be the expectation that they will be judged, assessed, guided or even cajoled into learning, and that it is properly someone else's function to decide what they should learn and how. The idea that they could be involved, at least to some extent, in making choices about their own learning may seem disconcerting to them at first. They may also resist the responsibility and commitment which this kind of training requires.

The trainer's initial task is to create a situation in which course members are willing to take what can seem to them to be a risk and dip their toes in the experiential water. The first step is to make clear right from the start the context and rationale for working experientially. Then the trainers can begin with relatively brief exercises like those described later in Chapters 2 and 3. These simple exercises keep anxiety levels to a minimum while enabling participants to experience the benefits of such methods. Individual resistance should be recognised without condemnation and responded to with empathy so that enough safety is created for course members to express their fears, apprehension and reluctance about this way of working. If the tutor is able to empathise with their discomfort and remain clear about the reasons for using this method, the sense of resistance usually abates pretty quickly. While it is important to give a clear rationale for the work, it is useful not to spend too long on this or get heavy-handed as the trainer can begin to sound defensive and anxiety levels can quickly rise again. It is probably most helpful to give a brief, clear instruction and outline (see pp. 31–2) and get on with the material so that people become emotionally involved before they have too much time to get anxious.

If, however, the group does start to seem 'stuck' in anxious or angry or resistant feelings, then the tutors will need to pay attention to the group process. Since there is a wealth of literature on this elsewhere, we are assuming that trainers who read this book will need only reminders rather than lengthy explanations of group process. Mary Connor's chapter on the dynamics of the training relationship in her book *Training the Counsellor* (Routledge, 1994) highlights common themes.

THE IMPORTANCE OF THE TRAINER–COURSE MEMBER RELATIONSHIP

On training courses the relationship between trainers and course members can have a powerful effect on the course outcomes and this is often thrown into high relief when experiential methods are used. If the trainers are able to respond empathically and then to highlight any parallels between the trainer–course member interaction and the counsellor–client interaction then the course has a rich additional resource upon which to draw. For example, tutors can remind course members of how they felt in the early stages of the course in order to explore the different reactions of clients to a counsellor who, counter to their expectations, is not telling them what to do.

Empathy is as important for the trainer as it is for the counsellor. She must be able to put herself into the shoes of the course member and assess the relevance of her training materials to him in his everyday work. The importance of this ability has been well established in the context of teaching and learning. The Aspy and Roebuck research of 1975 into effective teacher behaviour (*A Lever Long Enough*, Washington DC: National Consortium for Humanising Education, 1976) found the teacher's ability to communicate understanding of the world of the learner to be a significant factor in promoting positive learning outcomes. In Chapter 5 we show how case studies and role plays can be adapted to meet specific needs of course members.

The trainer must also be able to use her own authority wisely to maintain a firm boundary which can function as a container for the anxieties raised by these training methods. We know, of course, that anxiety and fear can be very close to excitement, and once course members begin to discover just what can be learned through case studies and role plays, they begin to get enormously excited. They may also discover new possibilities in their reading, their viewing and indeed in their relating beyond the confines of the course.

THE IMPORTANCE OF EQUAL OPPORTUNITIES

The 'end users' of counselling training are the future *clients* of course members. Many funding initiatives have been taken to attempt to make the range of helping services, including counselling services, available to all groups in our society; women and men from the full range of races, creeds and cultures; disabled and en-abled; gay, lesbian and 'straight'. Course providers, therefore, must make sure that course members are prepared for work with clients from this wide range.

At one time it was assumed that the emphasis on valuing and accepting people which is inherent in relationship training would be sufficient to enable course members to work with *any* clients. We now know that this is not the case and that unless prejudices and differences are specifically addressed in training, both course members and their clients will receive a poorer service. Very few, if any, course members would wish to treat one client better or worse than another. It is the unintentional behaviour, often born of assumptions of sameness which may never have been questioned, which relationship training seeks to address. This is also true for course tutors. Unless we have questioned our own assumptions, we are likely to treat course members (and hence their prospective clients) in covertly discriminating ways, however little we want or intend to do this.

One of the reasons why trainers may shy away from such material is that it can raise strong feelings in the whole group. Course members may become angry or fearful and respond by being combative or trying to deny that differences or discrimination exist. This is one of the many situations in which trainers can model the counselling approach, not denying but working *with* feelings and enabling course members to recognise the hurt and shame which may lie behind anger and defensiveness. Fortunately, there are now 'Training for Trainers' courses in counselling which can give trainers the support they need to tackle difficult issues such as these.

THE ELEMENTS WITHIN A TRAINING COURSE

The materials in this book have been written with the intention that they could be used in relationship training courses with a range of theoretical orientations. If, however, learners are to transfer their skills to a 'real-life' situation, they must be clear about their own theoretical framework so that they are able to make appropriate practice decisions. These materials are intended as an empowering tool for trainers, who are expected to use and interpret them within a training context which includes theory and personal development work, exercises and skills practice. In other words, case studies and role plays are very important methods but they do not, of themselves, constitute a complete training.

So what exactly are the elements of a training course that could train people to respond usefully to Mr Macduff?

There are three basic elements in counselling and psychotherapy training; development of knowledge and understanding, skills development and personal development. These three have a direct impact on the quality of a helping or therapeutic relationship.

Knowledge and understanding

Anyone using counselling skills or entering into a therapeutic relationship should have a clear understanding of *why* they are doing what they are doing in the way they are doing it. This understanding will come from a combination of:

- knowledge of the theory of personality development underlying the approach used;

- knowledge of common human psychological processes; bereavement, loss, marital interaction and so on;

- knowledge of the range of emotional responses which they and their peers have experienced in relation to events in their own lives;

- (at a more advanced level) knowledge of the causes and effects (as explained by their core approach and other approaches) of anxiety, depression, neurosis, isolation and so on.

Skills

Counsellors must also be sufficiently skilled to help others to deal with whatever is troubling them. This involves changing behaviour and usually entails a period of awkwardness and anxiety when course members have left behind some of their habitual ways of responding but have not yet become comfortable with new skills. The anxiety, if not the awkwardness, can be reduced if the tutor explains at the beginning of the course that this is likely to happen. The analogy of folding arms can be helpful:

> Fold your arms. Now fold them the other way. How does that feel? (Uncomfortable, weird, odd, awkward.) Counselling training is a bit like learning to fold your arms the new way. At first, you won't remember to do things differently. You'll automatically respond in the way you've always responded, without thinking. So we'll ask you to remind each other when you slip into old habits. Next, you'll try using your new skills and, because they're not part of *you* yet, you'll feel awkward and self-

conscious. We'll ask you to give each other a lot of support and feedback at this stage. Finally, you will be so used to using the new skills that you won't even think about it. They will just be a part of the way you operate.

Personal development

The importance of self-awareness in affective learning was outlined on page 9, where it was also recognised that, in order to be helpful to others, course members must be able to separate their own feelings from those of their clients. In the early stages of training, it is common for listeners to assume that their client's reactions to an event will be the same as their own. It is also common for much of the material covered on the course – loss, sexuality, ageing, violence and so on – to raise emotions in course members which could fruitfully be further explored.

Personal development is also important in two other respects. First, in experiencing the vulnerability of struggling with their own material and their own feelings, participants appreciate their future clients' struggles and the foundation is laid for ameliorating the power imbalance in the counsellor/client relationship. Second, course members learn to value the process by which they engage with their own discomfort and emerge feeling stronger and more self-reliant.

Most courses are structured to provide opportunities for individuals to explore their own feelings and experiences evoked by course material, usually through a personal development group of some kind with a skilled facilitator. Such a group cannot, however, provide ongoing counselling therapy and it is useful if tutors have a list of therapists and counselling agencies for people who wish to spend more time on their individual needs. More advanced courses usually expect course members to have or to have had their own counselling or therapy outside the course.

Combining these elements

For the trainer, it is neither possible nor desirable to separate totally the elements of theoretical understanding, skills development and personal development. Successful relationship training is multi-layered and interleaved. For example, in order to work effectively with someone who has experienced a loss, the helper or counsellor must, as a minimum;

- understand the patterns and processes of mourning (the reaction to loss);

- be able to relate these to the story of the individual with whom they are working;

- be able to communicate their empathy with and acceptance to that person;

- have explored their own losses and griefs in order not to confuse their own material with that of the other person.

As course members are taught about the processes of mourning, they are given opportunities to make the links with their own experience. As they explore their own experiences of loss and their own emotional responses they are supported by the empathy and acceptance of other course members. In turn, they use and develop their own counselling skills in supporting other course members' exploration.

Users of counselling skills, in common with therapeutic counsellors and psychotherapists, have the need to understand and work with the interrelationship between thoughts, behaviour and feelings. The effect of emotional responses on decision-making and behaviour, often neglected in the past, is increasingly understood. Our focus on affective development in this book does not mean that cognitive and behavioural aspects of human communication are less important. Training methods which promote development in all three areas are now used more widely.

Table 1 shows how cognitive, affective and behavioural development are integrated through case discussion and role play.

Table 1 Strands of development

	Cognitive development	*Affective development*	*Behavioural development*
Case study discussion	Hearing others' reactions to material leads to understanding of the range of possible responses.	Increasing willingness to accept other course members and clients unconditionally.	Practice in listening. Practice in formulating verbal responses to client material.
	Noticing own reactions leads to more and more sophisticated understanding of present self in relation to past experience.	Increasing ability to access own affective response (feel as well as think). Increasing acceptance of self.	

	Tutor explanation of themes and processes (e.g. loss, depression) leads to recognition of practice implications of theory.		
Role play as client	Understanding of hesitancy, vulnerability, fear, willingness or reluctance to trust.	Role play partner's acceptance and empathy leads to increasing acceptance of self.	Increase in facility of expression of own thoughts and feelings (congruence).
	Tutor explanation of process leads to recognition of practice implications of acceptance, empathy, congruence.	Greater awareness of own affective world (and its triggers).	
Role play as counsellor	Client/observer feedback leads to recognition of messages conveyed by verbal and non-verbal responses.	Increasing willingness to accept others unconditionally.	Development of responding skills.
	Acknowledgement of present limitations.	Growing awareness of self and others.	
Role play as observer	Understanding of how appropriate responses lead to self-awareness and self-acceptance in clients.	Growing awareness of similarities and differences between own affective world and others.	Increasing ability to select and phrase appropriate feedback.
	Understanding of development within a single interview and over a period of time.		Increasing ability to focus on others' frames of reference.

CONCLUSION

Case studies and role plays, together with 'real-life' practice are essential to the 'doing' aspects of training. Without them, course members may have a very sophisticated understanding of what *needs* to be done in order to facilitate clients, but may not be able to do it. As was shown on pages 14–15 with the arm-folding analogy, course members may need many opportunities for practice and feedback in order to move from the early stages of self-conscious and awkward responses to the point where they are congruently facilitative with clients.

The materials in this book have been written with the intention that they could be used in relationship training courses with a range of theoretical orientations. If, however, learners are to transfer their skills to a 'real-life' situation, they must be clear about their own theoretical framework so that they are able to make appropriate practice decisions. The materials are intended as an empowering tool for trainers, who are expected to use and interpret them within a training context which includes theory and personal development work, exercises and skills practice. In other words, case materials and role play are very important methods but they do not, of themselves, constitute a complete training.

Further, case materials and role play in training enable course members to prepare for more difficult issues before they are encountered in practice. For example, in Part II, we give materials which raise ethical considerations – situations which may arise infrequently but which can throw an inexperienced practitioner off course. Dealing with and discussing these first in the protected environment of the course raises course members' confidence considerably, as well as enabling them to handle such issues sensitively and ethically when they do arise in practice.

Widespread recognition of the value of experiential training is relatively recent. It was in the 1980s that the field of relationship training expanded dramatically as employees, volunteers and managers in diverse occupations became aware of the value of counselling and counselling skills. Nurses, social workers, teachers, doctors, managers and other professionals in training often found, particularly when feelings and emotions were part of the picture, that their technical and problem-solving skills did not meet the needs of all their clients. Beyond the technical requirements of the job, they turned increasingly to counselling skills training to equip them to work more effectively with *people* and found that the skills they learned enhanced and complemented existing technical skills. As a consequence, many occupational training courses now include elements of counselling skills training.

One of the consequences of counselling skills training becoming more widely available has been a greater awareness of the role of the fully trained therapeutic counsellor. The nurse, teacher, social worker, doctor or youth worker using counselling skills effectively is able to make informed judgements about whether clients can be enabled to manage their situation through the current relationship, or whether they should be referred to a therapeutic counsellor.

In this chapter we have considered the place of case materials and role play in counselling training. In the next chapter we take a closer look at how case materials work to promote development and at how we might most effectively use them.

2

CASE MATERIAL:
PURPOSES AND PROCEDURE

PURPOSES OF CASE MATERIAL

In this book, the term 'case vignette' is used to cover a range of briefly described scenes, like that of Macduff, into which course members project their own experiences and attitudes through the use of imagination. Case materials used as a framework in this way can help develop the *understanding* needed by counsellors and psychotherapists, through the use of imagination, exploration and reflection. For this reason, the case study material you will find in Part II of this book rarely gives an extensive or detailed case history, but gives just enough information to set the imagination going. In speculating about the people described – what they might be feeling, what might be motivating them to act as they do – course members are drawing upon their own experiences and those of others close to them. The person described in the case material thus becomes human and in some sense created and therefore 'known'.

There seems to be a deep human longing to make emotional connections with the experiences of others. Our capacity to enter the world of the characters in *Coronation Street* or *Brookside*, much as the Greeks were able to enter the world of Sophocles' characters, seems to indicate our general ability to imagine, at least in part, the world of another. The Ancient Greeks recognised the therapeutic releasing of emotion in an audience, triggered by the actors' expression of feelings in their role, and called it 'catharsis'. A similar process is at work when we 'feel our way' into a case.

Through the use of case materials, which themselves could be likened to a minute section of a TV 'soap' or a Greek drama, the capacity to empathise with others can be evoked and developed. Each member of the training group is invited to imagine him or herself in the situation described, and his imaginative capacity to enter that feeling world can then be developed and trained. People who do not have at least a large lump in the throat, if not actual tears, when watching a 'weepy' might have some difficulty in empathising with others. When, however, the characters' predicament puts the listener in touch with feelings of his own which prevent him from continuing to watch the film, then it is probable that the story has touched a hidden grief. This grief will need some attention if it is not to be triggered again and again in response to similar stories, whether imaginary, as with films or books, or real, as in the case of a client wanting help. The person who does not respond emotionally at all to others' griefs and heartaches may well be someone who has been hurt so deeply that in order to carry on with his life he has blocked the hurt completely from his awareness and cannot bear to recognise a similar hurt in others.

It is obviously not appropriate that listeners, counsellors and psychotherapists use their clients' stories to discover more about their own feelings. Case materials offer a safer way of helping trainees to do this, and, in particular, to identify which areas of their own feelings might be indicating the need for attention, through group work on the training course or through individual counselling or therapy for themselves. People in the 'helping professions' are increasingly recognising the value of counselling in helping them to distinguish their own from their clients' feelings and thus keep their focus entirely on their clients' needs.

USES OF CASE MATERIAL IN DEVELOPING EMPATHY

A case vignette can be used as a framework into which course members project their own experiences and develop their imaginative and empathic capacities. They become able, through a leap of the imagination and through drawing upon their own experience of feelings, to enter and be moved by the world of another. Through discussing case study material, course members are able to develop their perceptions in relation to their own and others' feelings, and to further their understanding of theory and reactive processes. Then, imagining themselves as a listener or counsellor to the person described in the case study, they have time to think about a range of possible responses and to discuss them with others. Unlike role play, case study discussion does not put course members 'on the spot'. It is, however, a valuable preparation for role play.

It is important in training to grade case materials so that they are sufficiently challenging at each step without raising so many issues that the identification process is hampered or even stopped.

Let us first of all take a relatively straightforward case vignette such as that of Henry:

> Henry is a man of about 30 who tells you he has worked for his firm since he left school. His line manager called him into her office last week. She tried to explain why the firm had decided to make Henry redundant in ten weeks' time

For a training group considering loss for the first time, a simple case study with a single focus of anticipated loss should be sufficiently straightforward to allow some imagination of the feelings of loss.

The more complicated example of Paul below draws attention not only to the phenomenon of actual loss (Paul's job), but also to potential losses (his mother-in-law, the GCSEs and a possible house move) as well as to secrets in the family.

> Paul is a man of about 40 who has worked for his firm since he left school. Last week his line manager called him into her office. She tried to explain why the firm had decided to make Paul and a colleague redundant in ten weeks' time.
>
> One of Paul's children is coming up to GCSEs, his wife's mother is quite ill and he has not yet felt able to mention the redundancy at home. He asks you what he should do . . .

In considering this case vignette, course members can think about Paul's world and discover what they themselves and what others are *feeling* as they talk about Paul's situation. Such a case study may well remind them of events in their own life or the lives of others close to them and they may talk about the emotions involved there. These personal experiences help to illuminate the discussion about Paul and give insight into Paul's world. Further, by moving the focus from Paul to another member of his family, a course member might identify more closely with Paul's wife, say, or his manager. Course members can then notice what they are feeling in relation to Paul's wife, her mother, the children. They might become aware of judgements and preconceptions which could prevent them from listening to Paul, for example: 'His wife has a right to know', 'All this redundancy nowadays – the Government just doesn't care about ordinary people', and so on.

At this stage, the tutor will accept and validate all course members' reactions and responses, using reflecting and summarising skills. This is not always easy, particularly when course members are dismissive, rejecting or prejudiced. If they stray down a lengthy side-alley, the tutor can say something like, 'We seem to have moved quite a long way from Paul.'

The tutor can then ask course members to move from feeling to *thinking*. Depending on the objectives for the session, she may ask course members to notice how some of these reactions will help them to understand what is going on for Paul and how other reactions may distract them from listening. She may draw attention to how those suffering a loss themselves often struggle to listen to, or even notice, the losses of others. She may ask them to consider how the various feelings of different members of this family may be affecting the interactions between them. She may ask them to identify the different loss elements in this case study.

The next step will be for course members to imagine themselves as the person to whom Paul has turned for help. They can discuss possible responses to Paul's question about what he should do and consider the implications of each. Again, the role of the tutor is important in alerting course members to ways in which their responses may 'leak' their own opinions or judgements, or focus Paul on actions rather than feelings.

Either before or after using such a case vignette, the tutor can present explanatory material about loss processes, the different ways in which men and women respond to loss, or other research findings on loss and depression. Such material can be understood through the common context of Paul and any similar experiences which course members have recounted in the discussion.

It is important to notice the wealth of material in what may seem at first a short and simple case study. The role of the tutor in focusing the discussion and ensuring that the learning objectives are met cannot be overstated. In practice, it is often more productive to use a number of short case vignettes like that of Paul, rather than a single lengthy account – three to five seems to work well with most groups. The person or people described in a single case may seem to some course members to be remote from their own experience, whereas with three to five vignettes, the likelihood of all participants being involved is increased. In addition, course members can enhance the learning derived from the first vignette when considering the second (and so on). This usually takes about forty-five minutes. If more than one study is used, explanatory theoretical material should be introduced after all have been explored, rather than after each one.

Thus we can see how case materials can offer an opportunity to explore thoughts, feelings and identifications, and, where appropriate, link them with relevant theory.

PROCEDURE FOR CASE MATERIAL

If we assume that the relatively straightforward case of Henry (page 20) is appropriate for the level of the course, we could summarise the procedure as focusing initially on the feelings and other responses evoked in the course members, then moving towards considering Henry's feelings, and finally thinking about related learning.

We have decided to use the case study of Henry, as one of the training methods during this session. Here is how we might proceed, step by step.

Step 1 Rationale and learning context

Trainees should be given a brief and clear rationale for the use of imagination in training, this time through the use of case materials. Case vignettes offer the possibility of a balance between imagination (trying to imagine what it is like to be Henry) and distance (it is Henry, not me, who is losing his job). This can allow for feeling, then some thinking about feeling and then, depending on the key questions (see below) some formulation of possible responses to Henry.

Step 2 Objectives and outline

The use of these particular case vignettes at this point on the course might be to enable the following objectives to be met.

At the end of the session, course members will:

- know that similar events may evoke different responses in different people;

- be able to identify their own responses;

- be able to identify similarities and differences in their own and others' responses to the same situation;

- be willing to accept others' responses as valid;

- be able to word a reply to each case character which reflects content or feelings.

Step 3 Introducing the case vignettes

Each case can be introduced either through reading aloud, giving a handout, displaying on a flip chart or an overhead projector, or a combination of these. The advantage of a handout is that it can be taken by the individual and read privately.

Course members should be given clear instructions to read, imagine and feel their way into each case on their own for, say, two minutes.

Step 4 Key questions

If the trainer were simply to give out the printed vignettes, the group discussion might range far and wide down whatever paths group members felt inclined to follow. Key questions are designed to focus the discussion in order to meet training objectives. After they have read and considered each case study, course members might be invited to jot down notes in relation to the questions prior to the discussion.

Key question 1: If you were in this person's situation, what might be your own feelings?

Key question 2: How might this person be feeling?

Key question 3: How might you respond as a listener to this person?

Step 5 Discussing feelings and key questions

Depending upon the level of openness and competence of the group, course members could be invited to join into pairs, or into fours before going into the full group. Sometimes moving from twos through fours into the group can facilitate the stages of feeling, thinking about feeling and formulating a response. Either way it would be important for the tutor to focus on specific answers to the key questions.

> For Key question 1, the tutor could encourage trainees to talk about any similar experiences they or those close to them had had; to recognise their own fears, judgements and wishes. (In relation to Henry, these might be: 'What if this should happen to me?' 'Fancy putting up with a woman manager!' 'He should have changed jobs before.' 'I want to make it better for him.')

> For Key question 2, the tutor could encourage trainees to focus on feelings rather than to intellectualise, analyse or theorise. This question also gives trainees an opportunity to extend their range of feeling words (anxiety, apprehension, fear, terror, worry, irritation, crossness, anger, fury, etc.).

> For Key question 3, the tutor could ask course members, either individually or with a partner, to choose from their perceptions about the character's feelings and find a form of words which would communicate their understanding. The tutor and other course members might then give feedback.

Step 6 Summary of learning

Summarising the answers to the key questions will help to reinforce the learning in Step 5 and will also underline the movement from feeling towards thinking, in particular about a useful response to Henry.

Step 7 Emotional debriefing

The group will be invited to notice any feelings inside themselves evoked by the material and be encouraged to recognise these feelings as a valid response to the material, even when the connections to Henry's situation are not immediately obvious.

Summary procedure

Step 1: Rationale and learning context

Step 2: Objectives and outline

Step 3: Introducing the case vignettes

Step 4: Key questions

Step 5: Discussing feelings and key questions

Step 6: Summary of learning

Step 7: Emotional debriefing

In the next chapter we shall move on to consider the purpose of role plays and the procedure for basic role plays. Chapter 4 will deal with variations on the basic role play.

3

BASIC ROLE PLAY:
PURPOSE AND PROCEDURE

PURPOSE OF ROLE PLAY

As we have seen in the previous chapter, case vignettes are frameworks into which trainees can: (a) project their own experiences to develop their own imaginative and empathic capacities; and (b) think about and discuss different facilitative responses.

A role play can develop *skills* by inviting participants to engage with each other more directly and immediately through the use of roles. Rather than thinking about Macduff or Paul Smith, they 'become' Macduff or Paul Smith. And in 'becoming' Malcolm, Macduff's friend, or Paul Smith's personnel officer, they have an opportunity to *practise* facilitative responding.

Case materials give the course members plenty of time to explore perceptions, to arrive at understanding and to prepare responses. Role play asks them to perceive, understand and respond 'on the hoof', without the benefit of prior discussion. This they may find quite challenging at first and the skilled tutor will grade the role plays, beginning with simple instructions to the talker and listener and allowing only a few minutes for each role. Initially, course members are often tongue-tied or reach for habitual responses such as asking questions. As with any other sort of skills training, practice is needed to turn knowledge into useful outcomes. Any amount of perception and understanding, discovered through working with case materials, will be of little practical value to their clients unless it can be communicated. Role plays provide the practice in communicating.

For counselling skills users, role play enables them to practise their skills in a protected environment before they transfer them to their own work. In more advanced training, role plays complement the work which course members undertake on their practice placement. They are of continuing value because: (a) participants usually feel more able to take risks with peers than with 'real' clients; and (b) peers and tutors are able to give informed feedback.

PROJECTED AND PERSONAL ROLE PLAY: PARTICIPANT ROLES

In order to set up a role play there need to be at least two, and preferably three, roles. These three participant roles are: the client, the counsellor and the observer. In the examples we give above, the roles of client and, sometimes, counsellor, involve the players in taking on the life circumstances or the job role of another person. At other times, course members will simply be asked to talk about themselves from their own personal experience and respond as themselves using counselling skills. This is not, however, a social interaction since the talking and responding will be focused and purposeful and they will still take one of the three roles of client, counsellor and observer.

We have grouped all of these activities together because, for the trainer, the teaching and learning processes are similar. When course members draw upon their own personal material to work with, we shall call the activity a **personal role play**. When they are invited to 'be' someone else, we call it a **projected role play**.

A simple personal role play, using everyday material, is a non-threatening way to become familiar with this method. The brief to both partners should be simple and clear. For example: 'Partner A is going to talk about the ups and downs of the past week. Partner B is going to paraphrase and summarise. After five minutes, swap roles.'

The client role: personal role play

Selecting a piece of one's own experience is a good place to enter the feeling world of counselling. The client role player in a personal role play explores an aspect of his current life or a memory of experience rather than entering imaginatively into the world of another person. It is the most basic and yet in some ways the most challenging form of role play because it addresses the trainee's capacity to allow, listen to and gradually accept his own feelings with increasing tolerance and understanding. Exploring and accepting their own feelings is an important aspect of course members' developing empathy towards others.

Course members are invited to take something of their own experience, and to talk about it, as far as possible, without monitoring; associating as freely as possible without conscious control.

Before course members are asked to use their own experiences in role play, it is important that the tutor makes it clear that they have some real choice about the subject matter. They are asked to select from their own experience something which they are ready to talk about with the partner they are working with and something which will not overspill the time allocated to the exercise. However, in beginning to talk about something with an accepting and empathic partner, course members sometimes find that the material they selected goes deeper and raises more painful feelings than they had anticipated. For example, a course member might choose to talk about the argument he had this morning with his teenage daughter. In becoming more aware of his feelings, he might begin to recognise uncertainties about himself as a parent, or even suddenly to remember unresolved hurts from his own adolescence. It is essential that course members have access to skilled help themselves in case the feelings evoked cannot be contained within the exercise – from a facilitator in a personal development group within the course structure or from their own counsellor or therapist.

By degrees, the trainers hand over responsibility to course members so that in the later stages of training the tutor simply announces a counselling practice of given length and whether or not there is to be an observer. Course members select something from their own experience to work on (often, but not necessarily, 'triggered' by the subject matter of a previous session) and manage the time between them.

The client role: projected role play

The role play of Macduff on page 7 is an example of a projected role play. It invites the conscious projection of the learner's feelings into the imagined situation; to 'be' Macduff. Many adults hesitate to take the leap into another role and there are, of course, limitations on how much we can ever manage to 'be' anyone else, and yet children, unless severely disturbed, seem to play quite easily at being 'mummies and daddies', 'doctors and nurses' and so on. The developmental power of play has long been recognised. Role playing draws on this capacity, often left largely dormant since childhood, of learning through doing. Through 'playing' at becoming the other person we can enter more directly their world as they experience it.

Such role plays require some 'trigger' material, and it is this kind of material which constitutes a large part of the resources in Part II of this book.

The counsellor role

The counsellor role offers course members the opportunity, first, to sense the feelings and try to understand the experience of another person; second, to monitor what is happening inside themselves; and third, and most importantly, to turn their perceptions and insights into skilled responses, which facilitate the exploration and development of the other person.

At the same time as participants in 'client' role explore their own experiences, those in 'counsellor' role learn to facilitate this process. In the early stages of training, the tutor will give them a clear and simple brief, enabling them to focus on each skill one by one, moving perhaps through listening, paraphrasing, reflecting feelings, beginning, ending, managing time, making a referral and so on as appropriate to their training.

Later, when such basic skills have become automatic, 'counsellors' are able to focus more on the process of the relationship. The value of the personal role play, particularly at early stages of training, is that the feedback given to the 'counsellor' is based on the actual reactions of the 'client' rather than on speculation about how an imagined client may have reacted.

Initially, of course, listeners are often so triggered into their own material that they react unknowingly, either by rushing in and being overwhelmed in an over-identification with the feeling or by denying the feeling altogether. This is a useful part of their overall learning. They begin to understand why self-awareness is so important in counselling as they appreciate how their own thoughts and feelings can interfere with their listening and responding to another person.

Section A of Part II gives materials which enable participants to practise beginning and ending sessions, making and receiving referrals, dealing with colleagues and managers and handling ethical issues.

The observer role

The observer role is primarily that of giving feedback to the 'counsellor'. The skills of giving feedback, particularly those of challenging appropriately, need to be developed. Since these are also important counselling skills, it is useful to spend some time preparing course members for the observer role and then revisiting the principles and practice of giving feedback at intervals throughout the course. Here is a possible reminder sheet for those learning how to give effective feedback.

GIVING AND RECEIVING EFFECTIVE FEEDBACK

Feedback helps us to learn about ourselves and the way we come across to others.

Receiving feedback gives us a chance to change and modify in order to communicate more effectively.

To be helpful, feedback needs to be given in a careful and supportive way.

Observations on helpful responses will reinforce good practice.

Observations on less helpful responses will provide opportunities for change.

Feedback should:

a) focus on the behaviour rather than the person (what s/he *does* rather than what we imagine s/he *is*);
b) use adverbs which relate to actions, rather than adjectives which relate to qualities;
c) contain observations rather than inferences (*what* is said or done, not *why* – our assumptions);
d) contain description rather than judgement;
e) be specific rather than general;
f) share ideas and information rather than giving advice (personalised – 'I felt, I thought...');
g) contain the amount of information the receiver can *use* rather than the amount we would like to give;
h) be concerned with behaviour the receiver can do something about.

It is useful to sandwich negative feedback between positives and check that the receiver hears both positive and negative.

When feedback has been given by several people, it is useful to give a summary of what has been said.

Source: Adapted from a training handout by Brigid Proctor and Francesca Inskipp.

Having paid attention to the whys and hows of giving feedback, tutors may then give the observer a particular brief according to the teaching point they wish to emphasise.

Examples:

Introductory course: How accurately did the listener paraphrase?
Role play on sexuality: Which areas tended to be avoided or distorted in this session?

In the later stages of training, the observer may also be briefed to facilitate the client giving feedback to the counsellor so that perceptions from inside and outside the role play are available to the course member.

PROCEDURE FOR BASIC PERSONAL ROLE PLAY

The following examples are of simple role plays from an introductory course, where it would be necessary to explain the procedure step by step. As course members become more familiar with the method, it will become unnecessary to repeat all of the details. We have used the terms 'talker' and 'listener' in these examples since they are taken specifically from counselling skills training.

Step 1: Rationale and learning context

This needs to be stated simply and clearly, as in the example below:

> We hope that at the end of this course you will be able to use some basic counselling skills in your work. To help you to do this, we're going to separate out each of the skills and spend some time on each. You will each have a chance to be the talker, so you can see how it feels from the receiving end, and the listener, so you can get some practice.

Step 2: Objectives and outline

The objectives emerge out of the rationale above, but are specific to the particular role play, rather than role play in general. Again, they can be usefully stated to course members, for example:

> The purpose of this role play is:
>
> (a) When you are listener, to notice how you usually respond. Do you

find yourself wanting to ask questions, for example? Do you want to talk about a similar experience of your own?

(b) When you are talker, to see what it feels like to be listened to attentively.

A very brief outline of the remaining steps can also be given at this point to set the framework for learning.

Step 3: 'A's tale'

Course members are asked to choose a partner whom they do not know, or know less well. All course members should be involved, making a threesome if there is an odd number of participants. A threesome is cumbersome but, on balance, likely to feel safer than working with a tutor. At this early stage of training the brief should be extremely clear and simple – for example:

> Decide who is A and who is B. A, you are going to talk for three minutes about some aspect of the ups and downs of last week. B, please listen but do not speak. You can nod and use facial expressions to show that you are listening. After three minutes I'll stop you.

As feelings begin to be addressed in the work, it is very easy for course members to become confused about such things as tasks and timing. It is therefore very important for the trainer to be extremely clear and succinct in the giving of instructions and to be both clear and firm about keeping to the allocated time. It is important that the feelings which emerge (whether from within themselves or evoked by another) be of manageable proportions so that a sense of confidence can grow. The amount of time therefore needs to be adjusted to the level of development and it is often surprising how much material can emerge in just three minutes. (A trainer might, of course, judge that either two or even six minutes would be more appropriate for the trainees at that particular stage.) A predictable and firmly held ending to the allotted time may feel frustrating for course members at first, but this clarity ultimately offers much greater safety. It also offers good modelling for counselling practice where the counsellor's capacity to hold clear time boundaries is such an important element in the safety of the therapeutic environment. When course members are talking and practising at this stage, an additional element of safety is given if tutors signal clearly, perhaps through obvious involvement with another task, that they are not surreptitiously 'listening in'.

After A has spoken and B has listened for three minutes a clear instruction to stop should be given.

Step 4: Letting go

A is then invited to try to let go of her own memories and feelings at that point so that she can be ready to attend to B. B is invited to let go of whatever memories or feelings were aroused by his listening to A and to begin to move back into the 'ups and downs' of his own week. At this stage about thirty seconds should be given for 'turn-around time' so that, whatever may have been aroused in B by the intensity with which A worked, B still has the option to work at the level which feels safe for him. The growing intensity with which the 'faster' trainees choose to explore their experiences will hopefully encourage the 'slower' ones to risk more; an important part of any group's development. This important 'turn-around time', however brief, helps to re-establish the conscious and deliberate level of work for the second partner.

Steps 5 and 6: 'B's tale' and letting go

B has then three minutes with A listening, and they are again then encouraged to let go of memories, feelings and role in order to look at the process.

Step 7: Exploration of the listening process

The exploration of listening and of being listened to is an extremely important part of learning and participants should be given plenty of time at this stage, say ten to fifteen minutes, to do this. The discussion should focus on the experience of listening and being listened to rather than the content of what was said and the discussion time should be clearly indicated. Course members are often tempted to identify with one another at this stage, 'Yes, it was just like that for me when I . . .', and they often need to be reminded that the learning here is about:

- the experience of having someone just 'shut up' and really listen, without having to worry about how the story is affecting them;

- the experience of actually listening to another while monitoring the difficulties of listening;

- the quality of listening, its effects upon both the talker and the listener and the intricate interactions between them.

Sometimes it is useful to join pairs into foursomes for a slightly wider discussion, and a greater emphasis on thinking, before moving into the larger group.

Step 8: Learning from the roles (group)

By asking well-prepared and clearly focused questions to the whole group, the tutor is able to summarise and reinforce the learning. For example:

> *For the client role*
> How was the experience of being listened to?
> What specific things enhanced or improved the feeling of being listened to?
> What things threatened to destroy that feeling of being listened to?
> If your listener had been allowed to talk, what would you have wanted from them?

> *For the counsellor role*
> As listener, were you tempted to speak?
> What kind of things might you have said? And in what ways might those things have been useful or not useful?
> What kind of things tempted you to switch off from listening?

In this way the purpose of the exercise is made clear and the main learning points (for example, anxiety about self-exploration and distraction to listening) can be summarised.

Because course members are different individuals and because they will not all have followed the brief equally well, they may have come to different conclusions at the end of the role play. Some, for example, may have enjoyed the attention of being listened to. Others may have been uncomfortable or embarrassed. In summarising, the tutor recognises the range of reactions and draws conclusions, for example:

> So, to summarise, many of you found that being listened to without interruption helped you to follow your own train of thought, but some of you wanted to be reassured that your partner understood what you were saying, and some of you 'dried up' and wanted a prompt to get you started again. We'll be looking at how you can do those things in next week's session.

Step 9: Emotional debriefing (group)

In Steps 7 and 8 trainees were being encouraged to move from feeling towards thinking, which included thinking about feeling. This capacity to notice and accept feelings and then to begin to move away from them towards considering the implications of an exercise and drawing concrete conclusions is an important aspect of the counsellor's development. After these 'thinking' steps, the group will be invited to notice any feelings they are still aware of which have been evoked by the material and will be encouraged to recognise these feelings as a valid response to the work of the exercise, even where the connections may not be immediately obvious. They will then be invited, individually, to 'let go' of any feelings which remain attached to the role and to be present, now, as learners in the group.

Step 10: Summary of learning (group)

The tutor should briefly summarise the learning in relation to the objectives stated at Step 2.

Summary of procedure for personal role play

Step 1: Rationale and learning context

Step 2: Objectives and outline

Step 3: 'A's tale' (B listening to A)

Step 4: Letting go (A of the feelings evoked by her memories, and B of the feelings evoked by A's story and by the listening role)

Steps 5 and 6: 'B's tale' and letting go (A listening to B)

Step 7: Exploration of the listening process (in twos and perhaps fours)

Step 8: Learning from the roles (group)

Step 9: Emotional debriefing (group)

Step 10: Summary of learning (group)

DEVELOPMENT OF PERSONAL ROLE PLAY AS TRAINING PROGRESSES

The example given above is of a personal role play used very early in relationship training. As course members develop other skills, their capacity to use this method also grows. They risk sharing deeper level material in 'client' role as the course progresses and they learn to give one another increasingly informed and courageous feedback. Gradually, the trainer hands over responsibility to course members so that in the later stages of training the task of the tutor is to observe that the work is going on and to respond to requests for assistance from course members. Course members select something from their own experience to work on and manage the time between them. The material they choose is often, but not necessarily, 'triggered' by a previous input session, so that a skills practice following an input on, say, sexuality or depression is likely to include material related to that theme.

This in turn develops skills and the ability to work with process in the corresponding counsellor role. Course members in this role are also working more and more in depth as the course progresses. As they become more confident with role play, the role of observer can be introduced to give additional feedback to the counsellor from 'outside' as well as 'inside' the interaction. They become more confident about recognising and dealing with their own emotions and thus more able to hear, respond to and contain the emotions of others. The advantage of personal role play over projected role play is that the 'counsellor' is responding to live, here-and-now issues.

PROCEDURE FOR BASIC PROJECTED ROLE PLAY

The procedure for projected role play is very similar to that for personal role play.

Step 1: rationale

As above, page 31.

Step 2: Objectives and outline

The objectives would be similar to those for personal role play, adapted as follows:

- to enter the feeling world of another (talker and listener role);

- to explore imaginatively the feeling world of another (talker role);

- to practise listening with full attention (listener role);

- to practise communicating understanding of the talker's feelings (listener role).

Step 3: Introducing the role

Let us assume that the role is as follows:

> You are a 30-year-old man called Henry and you have worked for your firm since you left school. Your line manager, Helen, called you into her office last week. She tried to explain why your firm has decided to make you redundant in ten weeks' time.

It is useful if course members have already done an attitude exercise, which may be based on case materials, to raise awareness of their own possible attitudinal difficulties in entering 'Henry's' world.

The role is most usefully presented as a written handout. Course members should be given time to read and absorb the role and then asked to put down their piece of paper before commencing the role play.

Step 4: Playing the role and responding

Client role: Course members should be given clear instructions to take, for example three minutes to read, think and imagine themselves into this role. They will then be invited to turn to their partners and to talk *as if they were Henry.*

Counsellor role: If there are particular skills which the trainer would like the listener to practise, or if there is a history to the talker role which it is important for the listener to know, then it would be useful to give the counsellor a written handout clarifying this. If not, and the listener is expected to respond to whatever she meets in 'Henry', then she might be invited, verbally, to centre herself to wait for her client.

Timing: Again it is very important for tutors to help course members (in both roles) to be clear and firm about the time allocated. This should be planned with the level of course members' development in mind. With experience, trainers will have a sense of how much time it will take members of this particular group to allow enough useful material to emerge or develop, without it being either overwhelming on the one hand or boring on the other. With more mature trainees it may be possible to be more flexible about timing, adjusting timing according to ways in which the role is used and developed. With early-stage trainees, however, it is important to give a clear finishing time and to stick to it.

Step 5: Discussing feelings and key questions

A lot of learning can emerge out of an apparently simple role play through paying attention to both roles. It is important, therefore, to give time to the experiences of both roles in responding to the key questions.

The key questions or tasks for this role might be:

- Did you discover attitudes or experiences in yourself which made it difficult for you to enter Henry's world? (talker role)

- What did you discover through entering Henry's world? (talker role)

- What, if anything, made it difficult for you to respond to your partner's 'Henry'? (listener role)

- What, if anything, was evoked in you by listening to 'Henry'? (listener role)

Step 6: Exploration of the listening process

Some exploration of the experience of listening will have happened at Stage 5. It is now important to focus on how the listening and responding of the counsellor affected Henry's experience at each stage and how this, in turn, may have affected the listener.

Step 7: Learning from the roles

In the group, through clearly focused questions, the learning from the different roles (and the interactive process) can be summarised:

- What specific things enhanced the experience of being listened to?

- What things threatened to destroy the experience of being listened to?

- What things were said which were useful?

- What things were said which could have been said more usefully?

- When might silence have been more useful?

- What might have been said which wasn't?

Step 8: Emotional debriefing

In Steps 6 and 7, course members are again encouraged to move from feeling towards thinking. For the projected role players it is particularly important that emotional debriefing enables the course members to leave the role behind. If any course members are having difficulty in completing this emotional finishing off, it is sometimes useful for them to talk to their partner about something mundane, spending two or three minutes in describing the training room, for example.

Step 9: Summary of learning

As for the personal role play it is useful to summarise the learning in relation to the objectives stated in Step 2.

TUTOR OBSERVATION

In contrast to their apprehension when first using role play as a method, course members quickly come to value feedback from course tutor observation. We have found that we need to be scrupulous about sharing our time evenly between triads. This is more possible over a period of time such as a term than during a single session and we tell course members at an early stage that they will not receive tutor feedback every session.

In this chapter we have looked at the purposes and procedures for basic role plays. In the next chapter we shall consider ways of working with a variety of more complex role play methods.

4

ROLE PLAY VARIATIONS

PURPOSE OF VARYING ROLE PLAY METHODS

Once the tutor and course members are familiar with and comfortable with basic role plays, they may wish to vary the method. Developing counselling skills is similar to developing any other skill; it is only with repetition that the course member moves from conscious incompetence, through conscious competence to the goal of unconscious competence, where the new behaviour is so integrated that it feels 'natural' to the user and receiver. It is the task of the trainer to vary the training methods so that skills practice is interesting and engaging rather than repetitious. These particular variations involve a larger number of people than the 'twosome' which is the norm for the counselling or counselling skills encounter, but the loss of intimacy can be set against the liveliness of these methods. The role play variations are summarised below and followed by more detailed instructions.

Horseshoe

This is a method of obtaining more experienced feedback on course members' counselling skills, used with a projected role play. The tutor is the role-player and a number of trainees, sitting around the tutor in a horseshoe formation, practise their skills and receive feedback from the tutor playing the role. Where the group is large or is relatively inexperienced, it is extremely useful to work with two tutors. In this case, feedback can be given from both 'inside' and 'outside' the role.

Excuse me

This method gives skills practice to a number of trainees working on the same material with the same 'client'. A course member plays a role and a number of players in turn slip into the counsellor role. The tutor and the rest of the group observe and can discuss and give feedback on the different skills and styles.

Rondelle

This method includes more course members as participants, but fewer external observers. A number of course members with the same role sit in an outward facing circle and an equal number of course members circulate around the outside, sitting down to use counselling skills with one particular role-player for between five and ten minutes before moving on to the next role-player.

Demonstration fishbowl

The training group sits in a circle around the role-players as a 'fishbowl' of observers. The roles (of counsellor and client) may be taken by tutors or course members (or one of each). Course members observe and then discuss the interaction, paying particular attention to the listener/counsellor responses.

Group and linked role play

Here, a number of course members are invited to enter different, but linked, roles such as those of a family. 'Family groups' can work on their own, or with a tutor–observer or with the rest of the learning group observing as in the Fishbowl. In this case, understanding can be intensified through having one or two course members 'double' (for instructions on this, see page 53) an individual in the group in order to pick up particular aspects of that role. Group and linked role play enables course members to explore and understand the effects of emotions on interactions within the group. Additionally, a facilitator or counsellor role may be introduced if course members' training includes couple or family therapy.

We shall now give more detailed procedural steps for those less familiar with these methods.

HORSESHOE

The horseshoe role play is invaluable in enabling course members to:

- Discuss responses to a developing situation.

- Hear three or four different responses.

- Hear tutor feedback to those responses.

This type of role play is particularly useful for tackling more challenging situations since there is a high level of support built in. It is very stimulating for the course members and very demanding for the course tutors. In particular, the tutor playing the client is switching in and out of role, trying to remember her reactions from 'inside' the role to three or four different responses and then facilitating discussion. She will, almost certainly, need to ask for a repetition of one or two responses. A second tutor, sitting to one side of the group, is a valuable additional resource.

The course tutor plays the client role and the group members are split into small groups of three or four arranged in a horseshoe around the tutor. One chair in each group faces the tutor, with two or three 'adviser' chairs behind.

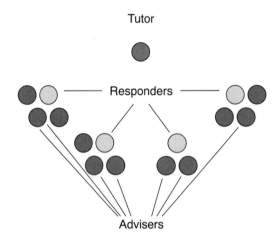

Step 1: Explaining the procedure

The tutor gives the following explanation:

> She is going to play a role and one person in each group will make a verbal response.
>
> The person in the responder chair will first discuss possible responses with his advisers. However, the decision rests with the responder, since each course member will have his own style of working and it is important to give feedback not only on what is expressed but how it is communicated.
>
> A role play such as this gives everyone the chance to experiment, take risks and find out how a different response might be received (which feels more dangerous when working with real clients). It is important not to see the exercise as simply a competition between the groups but to use any competitive feelings to help create a variety of responses.

Step 2: Introducing the role

The tutor tells the group:

> which role they are in (health visitor, manager, counsellor, psycho-therapist and so on);

> any background information they have about the person she will be role playing;

> which stage in the relationship will be dealt with in the role play ('This is the first time you have met me', 'You have been working with me for four sessions'...);

> which stage in the session will be dealt with in the role play ('We've been together about fifteen minutes and I've been telling you about...').

Step 3: Playing the role

The tutor begins in role, addressing herself to the responders seated in front of their advisers, for example:

> I don't know whether you can help me. In fact I feel a bit silly coming to see you like this. It's not a big 'problem' or anything like that, it's just I wanted to know something about old people's homes. Mum's getting so she can't really look after herself and she keeps coming to stay with me. Well I haven't really got the room, and David's getting fed up of having to sleep on the settee. Not that I mind having her, of course. Well, she's my mother, isn't she?

Step 4: Discussion

Responders have a discussion with their advisers. The tutor should allow five to ten minutes for this, since the discussion often takes in speculation about the client, previous teaching/learning points, giving support to anxious responders and so on. When it seems appropriate, she or the other tutor says, 'You have a minute left.'

Step 5: Responses

The tutor cues the responders by repeating the last role-play sentence or phrase and each makes his response in turn.

Step 6: Feedback

The tutor gives feedback from the role. This feedback should take account of the stage of training of the group and may relate to the content or the manner of the responses. For example:

> 'You said rather too much, for me. I couldn't take it all in. The first sentence was great on its own. Will you just say it again.'

> 'You were on the right lines but I felt a bit as though you were criticising me. It was the word "———" I reacted to. Perhaps you could phrase it differently. Does anyone have any suggestions?'

> 'Your warmth was coming through but you were using very academic language which was a bit intimidating. Could you say it in more everyday words? Can anyone else help?'

> 'I felt as though you really understood what I was saying. The word "———" was spot on.'

A second tutor here can take some of the pressure from the role-player by feeding back his/her own perceptions and asking questions of the role-player.

Step 7: Musical chairs move

The triads move round so that another person is in the 'responder' chair.

Step 8: Continuing the role

The role-player tutor chooses one of the responses and continues in role.
The process is then repeated from Step 3.

A Horseshoe role play takes from forty minutes to an hour. Since it is only possible to cover a small section of an interaction, the tutor may choose a middle or end section, describing, rather than role playing, the beginning.

In Part II of this book are a number of ideas for horseshoe roles. The roles are written as verbatim accounts to give the general flavour and not to suggest that tutors should memorise and repeat them as they stand. In fact, we would caution against this, since a lack of spontaneity on the part of the role-playing tutor will inhibit the responses of the course members. To a large extent, the development of the role will depend upon those responses. However, suggestions for development are given to be used if appropriate.

EXCUSE ME

This method of allowing several people to try out counselling responses is rather more spontaneous than the Horseshoe and is probably best introduced at a slightly later stage. In this method either a tutor or a course member plays an individual projected role and several other course members all take a turn at practising their counselling skills. The tutor needs to have more of a management role here to take charge of the timing. If playing the role herself, she should use a second tutor as time manager.

RONDELLE

With this method a larger number of course members play the same role, so that more people are actively involved, which raises the energy level but loses some of the observer feedback capacity. For a group of twelve, six course members (1–6) are given the same projected role and sit in an outward facing circle as shown below.

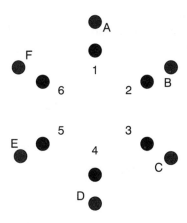

The other six members (A–F) sit down, as shown, with A opposite 1 and so on. Course members 1–6 all play the same role as given and A–F listen and use counselling skills. After a certain length of time, say five minutes, the tutor says 'Move on please' and A moves to 2, taking over from B. B moves to 3 and so on around the circle with F moving round to 1.

The feedback here is offered from the roles with the help of tutor observation. Course members 1–6 are given time to reflect upon the differences between and similarities of the responders and to note down feedback they wish to give to each. Course members A–F may be invited individually to note down their perceptions of the exercise or to discuss them as a group. They may, in particular, be asked to note how their ability to 'hear' each client's individual concerns was affected by the constraints of the exercise.

This is a particularly lively exercise but the level of frustration may also be high as the intimacy is constantly being broken.

DEMONSTRATION FISHBOWL

In this form of role play, the 'observer' role is extended to all course members who are not participants. The participants may be course members or tutors or one of each. The aim is for the whole group to discuss a common experience.

Participant chairs are set up in the centre of the room and the other members of the group arrange themselves in a circle around them. There may be a phase of the exercise where the other course members ask participants questions. If they are answering from the role, they should remain in the centre. Otherwise, they should move to become part of the circle and take part in the discussion as themselves.

This method can be used to demonstrate different possible responses to the same individual situation.

The client (personal or projected) and counsellor role players work together in the centre of a circle constituted by the other trainees who are the observers, as shown below:

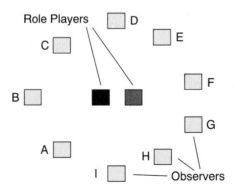

If the role is projected, the role player should be given a clear written role and be given time to get into that role. The person playing the counsellor role in this method may feel quite anxious and it is important to give clear instructions and support for the role.

It can also be useful, possibly as a development from basic general observation, to allocate specific aspects of observation to subgroups of observers. For instance observers A, D and G might be asked to focus on the body language of both role players, while B, E and H might be asked to look for demonstrations of empathy skills from the counsellor and their effect on the client, and observers C, F and I might be asked to look for challenging skills and their effects.

These specific observational tasks can be developed still further with the method of 'doubling' which is described on page 53.

GROUP AND LINKED ROLE PLAYS

You will remember from Chapter 1 that course members can play a number of linked roles in order to experience what it is like to be a member of a particular group and then to think about the dynamics of that group.

In linked role plays, there may or may not be a 'counsellor' or 'listener' role as part of the group. This will depend both on the context for learning and the level of course members. Some linked role plays in Part II do have a counsellor role and would normally be used only with learners who had considerable experience of role playing. With or without a counsellor role, this method can be used to enable learners to experience and understand more about dynamics *between* the different members of a group.

As an example of a role play we shall take Paul's family – the Smiths. There are four members of the Smith family: Paul, his wife Noreen and his children Kate and Geoff. There is also Noreen's mother, Mrs Mary McSweeny, who will at times be part of the group and at other times will not.

PAUL:

> You are a man of about 40 who has worked for your firm since you left school. Last week your line manager called you into her office. She tried to explain why the firm had decided to make you and your colleague redundant in ten weeks' time.
>
> One of your children is coming up to GCSEs, your wife's mother is quite ill and you have not yet felt able to mention the redundancy at home. You want someone to help you to decide what you should do ...

NOREEN:

> You are 43 and your mother (Mary), now over 70, is quite ill. She is due for a test at the hospital in three weeks' time but you sense she is going downhill quite fast. Your daughter's GCSEs start in two months. Your husband seems odd at the moment and you can't get through to him . . .

KATE:

> You are just 16 and your GCSEs start in eight and a half weeks' time. Your family are keen for you to do well. Your Gran (Mary) is not well at the moment but the doctor didn't seem to be that worried. Your mum and dad have both, in their own ways, been acting rather strangely and you wonder if they've been having a row. You wish they'd leave you in peace to get on with your work . . .

GEOFF:

> You are 14 and have just been passed over as a member of your local junior football team. Your family used to be supportive of your sporting interests but now they seem to be ignoring you. You know you should be thinking about your GCSE subject choices but you don't seem to be able to work up much interest. You wonder whether your parents are upset with you . . .

and sometimes there is . . .

MARY:

> You are over 70 and have not been feeling well for nearly a year now. Just recently you've been having considerable pain in your abdomen and your appetite continues to decrease. You wonder how long you've got. Your son-in-law Paul seems moody and your daughter Noreen seems distracted. You wonder whether they have been having a row . . .

The tutor can structure this family role play in two ways:

- Asking participants to interact as a family group:

    (a) with tutor as observer;
    (b) with a general Fishbowl of observers;
    (c) with specific 'doubles' in a Fishbowl formation (see page 53).

- Taking individuals out of the family context into specific, different role-played counselling situations.

When working with this group as a family it is important to highlight that group members' learning occurs through letting themselves experience being members of this group (family) and noticing what it is like to be part of that interlinked group. Further learning can then later occur through listening to each individual member's experiences of being a part of that group, whatever the method of observation.

In this case the tutor would hand out the roles, give time for each individual to think and feel his way into the role and then invite all the role-players to join up and become a part of this family. Other members of the group can make suggestions about the setting and context for the family. Those experienced in role play should not find it too difficult to enter the roles but it may take time for the family to 'get going'.

Once the family interactions have been played for a while – somewhere between ten and twenty minutes – the 'play' should be stopped and the tutor address certain key questions to the players *while they are still in role*, for example:

- What feelings do you experience as part of this family group?

- What are your feelings towards other members of your family?

- What thoughts do you have about other members of your family?

- What things did you find it difficult to say just then in the family?

- What things did you find it difficult to say just then to specific people?

Once the experiences of the family have been thoroughly explored in role, it is important to debrief emotionally and de-role each participant. Since the process, by now, will be familiar, other members of the group can be asked to help with this.

Once members have been debriefed, further questions can be addressed from outside the roles, for example:

- What things did this family find easy to talk about?

- What things did this family find it difficult to talk about?

These questions can also be addressed as key questions to a general Fishbowl of observers round the outside of the family, as well as any general observer questions. It can be useful to ascribe specific observer roles to individuals either in the method outlined for the demonstration Fishbowl (page 46) or by ascribing the observation role per role-player so that each has a 'double' as described on page 53.

Once the doubles have all been given a chance to 'round out' the perceptions from the roles, then a pattern of interaction may emerge which throws light on families' reactions to loss and the possible areas of work of counsellors working with individuals from a family which has suffered loss, or potential loss, and where patterns of denial have set in. It can then be useful to set up role plays for each individual with a counsellor/listener in a separate and different context.

General Practice context

NOREEN SMITH:

> You are 43 and your mother (Mary), now over 70, is quite ill. She is due for a test at the hospital in three weeks' time but you sense she is going downhill quite fast. Your daughter's GCSEs start in two months. Your husband seems odd at the moment and you can't get through to him. You've gone to your GP to see if you can get the hospital appointment for your mum brought forward ...

GP:

> Mrs Smith has come to you about her mother's hospital appointment. You would also like to bring the appointment forward if you can, but you are sensing that there are other things which Mrs Smith may want to talk about ...

Hospital context

MARY MCSWEENY:

> You are over 70 and have not been feeling well for nearly a year now. Just recently you've been having considerable pain in your abdomen and your appetite continues to decrease. You wonder how long you've got. Your son-in-law Paul seems moody and your daughter Noreen seems distracted. You wonder whether they have been having a row.
>
> You have come to the hospital for your tests. You are of course anxious about the tests, but you are also puzzled about what's going on at home and you think they may know something you don't know. You think this nurse looks understanding and you want to try and talk to her about things at home ...

NURSE:

> Mrs McSweeny's tests give a reasonable prognosis but you're not sure it's the tests she really wants to talk about ...

School context 1

KATE:

> You are just 16 and your GCSEs start in eight and a half weeks' time. Your family are keen for you to do well. Your Gran (Mary) is not well at the moment but the doctor didn't seem to be that worried. Your mum and dad have both, in their own ways, been acting rather strangely and you wonder if they've been having a row. You wish they'd leave you in peace to get on with your work.
>
> You're beginning to feel really anxious about your ability to get through your revision schedule with the troubles at home and you've come to see your Year Tutor about things ...

YEAR TUTOR:

> Kate is a well-organised student who is expected to do well. You've heard from her English tutor that she's been less organised recently ...

School context 2

GEOFF:

> You are 14 and have just been passed over as a member of your local junior football team. Your family used to be supportive of your sporting interests but now they seem to be ignoring you. You know you should be thinking about your GCSE subject choices but you don't seem to be able to work up much interest. You wonder whether your parents are upset with you ...
>
> You've been asked to go and see your Form Tutor ...

FORM TUTOR:

> You are dimly aware from the last parents' evening that Geoff's Gran has been ill, but you're not sure why he is suddenly causing his teachers such distress ...

Work context

PAUL:

> You are a 40-year-old man and you have worked for the same firm since you left school. Last week your line manager called you into her office and tried to explain to you why the firm were making you and a colleague redundant in ten weeks' time.
>
> Your daughter Kate starts her GCSEs in eight and a half weeks' time, your wife Noreen's mother is quite ill, you haven't seen Geoff (14) for days and you haven't quite dared bring up the subject of your redundancy at home yet. You've come to see the personnel officer about the terms of your redundancy, you're not sure if she'd under-stand about the family...

PERSONNEL OFFICER:

> You met Paul Smith at a firm's outing and found him calm and pleasant. You realise that redundancy is never an easy matter but Paul seems particularly distracted this morning...

VARIATIONS ON THE VARIATIONS

For all of the methods described above, there are additional training techniques which can add to the learning.

Freeze frame

This is a technique by which the tutor and, later, course members themselves can stop a role play in the middle for discussion to take place. The tutor has an imaginary remote control which acts upon the role play as though it were a video recording. It is particularly useful during a Fishbowl or other observed role play if a course member in counsellor role seems to be struggling, since learning is not helped by lists of negative feedback. Once the tutor has called 'freeze frame', she can ask the observers to discuss what they see happening or to offer helpful suggestions to the 'counsellor'. During this, the role-players simply listen and the role play resumes when the tutor calls 'play'. The tutor can also 'rewind' to give the role-players a chance to try a different approach from a given point in the interaction. (See also Michael Jacobs, *Insight and Experience*, Open University Press, Milton Keynes, 1992, for a description of a similar technique which Jacobs calls 'time out'.)

Doubling

Any role can be assisted by a 'double' whose aim is to get in touch with feelings in the role-player which are 'just below the surface'. These insights can be used in two ways.

First, an 'observer double' can be asked questions in the debriefing phase such as 'What feelings do *you* think Geoff was having difficulty noticing [or expressing]?' It is important to give each double the opportunity to address the question while the original role-player is still in role, as he or she may then be able to get in touch with feelings which were just under the surface and which, once addressed, will be easier to 'get rid of' in the debriefing session. If a particular role-player finds it difficult to recognise in himself feelings which appear to be accurate from the double, then this may indicate aspects of denial in the role-playing course member himself and should be addressed in self-awareness sessions (see pp. 9–10).

Second, an 'active double' can express such feelings at the time, as if he were in the role. A double who is picking up angry feelings in the role-player might say as if in the role himself, 'I'm very angry with you.' If the role-player is indeed experiencing angry feelings, he will repeat the statement using his own words. If he is not, he will simply ignore the intervention.

Stakeholders

Another role for an observer can be that of someone who would not be present during an interaction such as a counselling session, but who would have views and feelings about what is taking place. This may be a partner, family member, colleague, supervisor and so on. A course member is asked to observe as though they were that person and contribute that person's feelings prior to the overall debriefing. Tutors should take care to ensure that this is a separate phase, so that it does not 'muddy' the original role play. Any number of stakeholders can be used, with the stakeholder group having a separate discussion in role. In the debriefing, the tutor can enable the group to explore issues such as responsibilities, boundaries and ethics.

Video and audio recording

Many courses now have facilities for course members to tape record and play back their interactions. Initially, many course members find this worrying and tutors can help by emphasising that the recording is the property of the people who make it. It is for them to decide whether or not to view the tape and if they feel embarrassed by what is recorded they may choose simply to wipe it. If they decide to view or listen to it, they can do so in private (and then wipe it if they wish), or seek comments from peers or course tutors. The importance of tapes to learning is that the resulting information is not filtered through anyone else's perceptions in the way that 'live' observer feedback is. Hence it is less easy to deny or distort.

As the training progresses, course members become more at ease with hearing and seeing themselves on tape. Tutors can then be involved in helping course members to recognise and understand what was happening and in suggesting ways in which the 'counsellor' could have been more facilitative. Advanced courses usually have regular opportunities for this, in small groups and on a one-to-one basis, often as part of a formative assessment process.

Interpersonal Process Recall

Interpersonal Process Recall is a technique for illuminating the counselling process. A tape is played back to the participants by a neutral third person called the 'inquirer'. Either participant may stop the tape at any time when reminded of their inner thoughts and feelings during the original interaction. The inquirer helps them to explore and clarify these and so become more aware of how their overt responses were affected by them. The distancing effect of discussing a recording and the non-judgemental stance of the inquirer often enable participants to be very open about their inner worlds and to draw significant conclusions about their counselling practice. (See Norman I. Kagan and Henya Kagan, 'Interpersonal Process Recall' in P.N. Dowrick and associates, *Practical Guide to Using Video in the Behavioral Sciences*, Wiley, Canada, 1991.)

CONCLUSION

The main point of creating all these roles and case studies is to give course members the chance to practise their counselling skills in a variety of situations, receive feedback (in and out of role) from a variety of 'observers' and then practise their skills again. In practising their own skills with consistent observation and feedback, while at the same time honing their own observation and feedback skills through watching others and hearing other observers, they will learn more and more about the counselling relationship.

How to adapt case studies and role plays for different levels and different contexts will be addressed in the next chapter.

5

ADAPTING CASE
AND ROLE PLAY MATERIALS

INTRODUCTION

A basic case vignette or role play comprises items of information which enable learners to identify with a potential client's world, to discuss theory in relation to practice and to obtain feedback on their own practice. These 'items of information' can be adapted to make the material simpler or more complex, depending on the level of training. They can also be adapted to reflect the different work contexts of course members and the range of different client groups.

This chapter starts by giving a synopsis of different training levels and shows how the same material can be adapted for the different training levels through the use of different key questions. Following that, examples are given of how the material itself can be adapted for a range of purposes. Then follows a section on how to adapt materials to the working contexts of both homogeneous and heterogeneous groups and to contexts requiring management and authority skills. The chapter ends with a brief section on the importance of using case materials which recognise differences between people and allow exploration of discrimination.

LEVELS OF TRAINING

The following are the four broad categories generally used at present to describe different levels of training:

Introduction to counselling

An introduction to counselling is usually a course of between fifteen and thirty hours. At the end of such a course, participants can expect:

- to know the difference between counselling and counselling skills and other related activities such as advice, guidance and befriending (see J. Russell, G.

Dexter and T. Bond, *Differentiation between Advice, Guidance, Befriending, Counselling Skills and Counselling*, Dept of Employment, 1992);

- to know that there are a number of different 'schools' of counselling and to be clear about which approach the trainer is taking;

- to be able to use some basic listening skills.

Certificate in counselling skills

A Certificate in Counselling Skills course usually takes at least a year, with a weekly session of three or four hours and a residential component. At the end of such a course, participants can expect:

- to be able to use a range of counselling skills within their main role – teacher, nurse, welfare rights adviser, telephone helpline worker and so on;

- to know the theoretical framework which underpins the course approach – person-centred, gestalt, psychodynamic and so on;

- to know something of other theories;

- to be aware of their own responses, values and individual prejudices;

- to know and work within an appropriate Code of Ethics and Practice (usually that of the British Association for Counselling).

Diploma in counselling or psychotherapy

A full Diploma training is at least one year full-time or two to four years at one or two days per week, plus a residential element and supervised work practice. At the end of the course, participants can expect:

- to be able to work in depth, creating and maintaining a therapeutic counselling relationship;

- to have a thorough understanding of the theory of personality development which underpins the course practice;

- to understand other theories and recognise the similarities and differences;

- to understand and be able to work with common processes such as those triggered by loss, particularly where such processes are complicated by other factors;

- to understand the causes of emotional distress, disturbance and dysfunction and be able to make appropriate practice decisions.

Courses at this level have a supervised work practice element.

Higher degrees in counselling or psychotherapy

Higher degrees in counselling and psychotherapy are a relatively recent phenomenon. In line with other higher degrees, they tend to focus on the research and theoretical aspects of the work and are not intended primarily to be practitioner training. This, however, has raised some concern that participants with little or no practice experience may be employed as practitioners on the strength of an MSc or PhD. (See also C. Scanlon and A. P. Baillie, 1994, 'A preparation for practice?', in *Counselling Psychology* 7.4, pp. 407–27.) Courses are increasingly insisting on a Diploma training or equivalent as an entry requirement.

National Vocational Qualifications

National Vocational Qualifications (NVQs) in counselling and psychotherapy are being developed currently. The process involves practitioners, their employers and their professional organisations such as the British Association for Counselling and the United Kingdom Council for Psychotherapy.

One of the potential advantages of NVQs is that they are concerned with competence (which is defined as the combination of knowledge, skills and attitudes necessary to doing an effective job) rather than with the methods of achieving competence. It is left to the professional judgement of the trainer to make decisions about the content, methods and so on. As a result, any of the above courses may lead to an NVQ at the appropriate level, irrespective of differences in content or methodology or hours in the course. So, too, may learning through other routes: a combination of reading, short courses, supervision and learning from colleagues, for example. To obtain the qualification, candidates must demonstrate their competence in the areas specified.

There are some concerns among trainers that NVQs in such complex fields as counselling and psychotherapy may be difficult to operate and that the subtle, intuitive responses which characterise skilled relationship work cannot be 'reduced to mere' competences. However, it seems to us that the philosophy of NVQs has much to recommend it. Our own commitment is to the development of good training practice and our hope is that the work towards definition of competences will contribute to this.

USE OF KEY QUESTIONS FOR DIFFERENT OBJECTIVES

It is possible, through the use of focused questions, to evoke different learning from the same role play. In the resources section at Part II we have classified material according to theme but, in using this theme material, the trainer will need to adapt the key questions to take account of the session objectives and the needs of the particular training group. Here is an example:

> Henry is a man of about 30 who tells you he has worked for his firm since he left school. His line manager called him into her office last week. She tried to explain why the firm had decided to make him redundant.

Here is an example of how the case vignette of Henry could be used in meeting different objectives on different courses:

COURSE A:

INTRODUCTION TO COUNSELLING

Objective: To recognise trainee's own feelings in response to this situation as separate from those of Henry.

Key question 1:

If Henry approached you for help in this situation, what might be your own feelings?

> *Tutor encouragement to recognise:* Helper judgements (He shouldn't be angry; it's about time he had a move); fears (Help! What should I do now?) (We've found him a job. What more can he want?); wishes (I want to make it better for him).

Key question 2:

How might Henry be feeling?

> *Tutor encouragement to:* Focus on feelings (tutor feedback to course members who analyse, theorise, intellectualise etc.); recognise which feelings might belong to Henry and which to course members.

Relevant theoretical material: Frames of reference; recognition of the non-judgemental therapeutic position.

COURSE B:

CERTIFICATE IN COUNSELLING SKILLS

Objective: To explore the concept of empathy.

Key question 1:

Think yourself into this person's frame of reference. How might he be feeling?

Key question 2:

What might be making it difficult for you really to listen to Henry's feelings?

Key question 3:

As the listener, how might you reflect back this client's feelings?

Relevant theoretical material: Empathic listening and responding; difficulties in moving into and working within another person's frame of reference.

COURSE C:

CERTIFICATE IN COUNSELLING SKILLS FOR THOSE WORKING WITH LOSS AND GRIEF

Objective: To understand the reactive processes following loss.

Key question 1:

Looking at common reactions following loss, what range of feelings is Henry likely to be experiencing?

Key question 2:

What are the possible ramifications of this loss for Henry?

Key question 3:

How can a listener be most helpful to Henry?

Relevant theoretical material: Theories about loss, grief and the mourning process; the factors affecting loss.

Diploma level

The case vignette of Henry is less likely to be useful at Diploma level. If, however, course members, considering more complicated loss and grief, have lost sight of and need to revisit basic principles and practice, this is one of a number of vignettes which could be used (others can be found in Part II, Section B). At this level, significant practice development takes place in supervision, where course members, facilitated by an experienced counsellor, consider their ongoing therapeutic relationships. Diploma courses usually have training supervision built in to the course structure, often in small groups where the supervisors may also be members of staff involved in teaching and assessing. Other courses offer individual supervision outside of the teaching and assessment structure of the course. On these courses there are usually Case Groups or Counselling Presentation Groups for integrating theory and practice.

Within both of these systems there are still many occasions on which training objectives are best met through using role play or case materials, either in the Case or Supervision Group or the full training group. One example would be of a trainer using case materials to address complex ethical issues which course members might have to address in their work practice. Another example would be where a supervisor helps a course member to express something which he wants to communicate to a client. The supervisor may simply suggest that he role plays with another supervisee: 'Try saying it to Nilam.' Supervisees familiar with role play methods will slip into this quite naturally.

It is at this level of training that trainers often find it particularly useful to create their own appropriate materials. For instance, if a number of course members are experiencing similar difficulties in their work practice, the trainer could construct appropriate case materials or role plays to help deal with these – a more effective and economical approach than tackling each individual instance. Examples of this might be when a number of clients are failing to turn up to sessions, or are being passive with respect to the counselling process.

ALTERING THE COMPLEXITY OF THE MATERIAL

It is possible to adapt almost any given case study or role play to a lower or simpler level of training or to a higher and more complex one, according to the learning objectives. We indicated this process briefly on page 37, when we simplified the 'Paul' case vignette with its many different aspects of loss for different and related people, to the vignette of Henry, where the focus was on one (apparent) loss for one person, rather than a number of losses for different people all impacting on one another.

> Henry is a man of about 30 who tells you he has worked for his firm since he left school. His line manager called him into her office last week. She tried to explain why the firm had decided to make him redundant.

For the course tutor, it is important to try to decide which are the elements in the material necessary to achieve the desired objectives. If, for instance, the objectives are: (a) to enable course members to recognise losses in human life; and (b) to work with situations of loss by allowing space for the 'loss feelings', then four or five relatively simple case vignettes such as that of Henry (above) would be enough to explore the elements of loss and range of likely feelings. They could also trigger discussion about the grieving process and the value of expressing angry feelings in words.

Once the group had used the simple case vignette of Henry to explore and understand loss and grief, they could move on to practise the skills expected of them in a helping role. Such a 'helping role' might be that of a personnel officer using counselling skills. The skills of responding to Henry could then be practised using role plays as follows:

HENRY:

> You are a man of about 30 and have worked for your firm since you left school. Your line manager called you into her office last week. She tried to explain why the firm had decided to make you redundant in ten weeks' time.

PERSONNEL OFFICER USING COUNSELLING SKILLS:

> Henry has just come to see you to talk about his forthcoming redundancy. You are aware that Henry might be very hurt about this redundancy and may well be hiding his angry feelings from you, as someone with a responsible post in the organisation, even though he knows that you yourself are not responsible for the actual redundancy. You know the value of his expressing his feelings, if only he can feel safe enough to do so ...

It is important to create or to use materials which are *no more complicated* than they need to be to achieve the required objectives. In Part II we have attempted to grade the resource materials so that the 'simplest' come first in any given section. Such 'simple' loss materials can easily be adapted to increase the level of complexity and raise awareness of multiple losses.

Let us, for instance, assume that there are no other jobs for Henry in his area and in order to find another job he would have to move to a different part of the country. Course members can then be alerted to the fact that the loss constituted by redundancy may bring other losses in its train, such as loss of friends, neighbourhood, school, security and so on.

Similar vignettes can be used to develop recognition of less obvious losses. If, for instance, Edwina, rather than being made redundant, were being promoted to a different part of the country, then she would still be suffering the loss of friends, neighbourhood and so on, but in this case these losses might easily be ignored in the excitement of the promotion. This material could be particularly useful at an early stage of training in meeting the objective of enabling course members to recognise losses which are easily overlooked. Relocation might be an 'easy' loss for course members to imagine or think about for themselves and such a case vignette or set of role plays would be useful to those on a shortish course designed for managers associated with relocation.

If course members are then asked to take into consideration that Edwina might have a family, they will see that even though the promotion may offer the family greater financial security, the losses of home, friends, neighbours and proximity to relatives are likely to have a significant impact.

The roles begin to look a bit more complex:

EDWINA:

> You are a woman of about 35 and you have worked for your firm in Exchester, your home town, since you left school. The branch in Exchester is closing down and your line manager has been able to move you to a promoted post in Wyborough which is about 300 miles away. You have been having severe difficulties in your marriage recently and you have at last got an appointment to start Relate counselling. Also, your son has just received a scarce place in a local school for special needs children. Your new job starts in ten weeks and you have been asked to come and see the personnel officer about relocation arrangements.

PERSONNEL OFFICER (Exchester):

> You are a personnel officer for a firm whose branch in Exchester is closing down. Edwina is a woman of about 35 who tells you she has worked in Exchester, her home town, since she left school. Her line manager has been able to move her to a promoted post in Wyborough, some 300 miles away. The new job starts in ten weeks. Edwina has been advised by her line manager to come and talk with you about the help available for relocation, but you sense that she is feeling rather

overwhelmed by her family's reaction to the move, and a bit guilty about her own mixed feelings.

The excitement about Edwina's promotion, and perhaps also the relief of greater financial security, may cover a lot of anxieties about other potential personal losses which might not have been immediately obvious to the personnel officer.

While Edwina's losses are at least balanced by some gains, Paul Smith's losses seem all too obvious.

PAUL SMITH:

> Paul is a man of about 40 who tells you he has worked for his firm since he left school. His line manager called him into her office last week. She tried to explain why the firm had decided to make Paul redundant in ten weeks' time.
>
> One of Paul's three children is coming up to GCSEs, his wife Noreen's mother is quite ill and he hasn't yet felt able to mention the redundancy at home. He asks you what he should do.

Course members working with the range of losses in this case vignette can be invited to imagine the sense of crisis which Paul might be experiencing. Paul has suddenly been presented with a situation of (potential) loss over which, it seems, he has no control. We do not know what this loss actually means for Paul. It is likely to mean loss of income and loss of financial security. It may also mean loss of status, loss of pride, loss of sense of self, loss of bread-winner role. Furthermore, we do not know what possibilities there are in Paul's position of ultimately finding a similar – or even better – job, but it is likely that, for the moment, he is feeling shocked and probably powerless and disoriented. He may be feeling angry or helpless or guilty... or all of these. There is a whole range of feelings and dilemmas for course members to explore and think about within the realm of Paul's experience, before creating role plays to practise the skills of responding to Paul. The person playing Paul's role might decide that Paul is not used to expressing his feelings openly, especially when he is experiencing his feelings as somewhat overwhelming. Paul may be thinking that he cannot tell the family and 'add to their troubles'. This may, of course, be his way of protecting himself from letting himself experience his more 'difficult' feelings such as guilt or helplessness.

Paul's family members are also facing additional potential losses and crises. His wife, Noreen, may be facing the death of her own mother. Her mother is facing her own illness and, perhaps, death. Daughter Kate is facing the 'crisis' of GCSEs and poor Geoff's 'crisis' of the football team may seem, to some, utterly unimportant beside the others.

We could add to Paul's family situation the following elements:

Emerging homosexual feelings in his 14-year-old son Geoff.

Clear signs of senile dementia in Mrs McSweeny, the grandmother, who obstinately refuses either to go into a home or to stay with the family.

Clearly, this level of complexity would be much more appropriate for a group which already had a sophisticated understanding of loss, change and grief and which was familiar with role play as a method.

Thus, in summary, course members can be engaged with the same basic situation in a number of different ways. Discussing the information in case vignettes raises their awareness of loss and enables them to explore aspects of relevant theory and practice. Role plays of Paul and, say, a personnel officer, would allow them to practise responding to Paul. Participating in a group, linked role play, would involve them in a series of complex interactions, with different people imagining a range of feelings in response to the separate losses described, and then reacting and responding accordingly.

ADAPTING FOR DIFFERENT WORK CONTEXTS

Having considered differences in complexity, we shall go on to look at how materials can be adapted for different contexts. The contexts in which people are helped through the use of counselling skills are very varied and it is difficult to overestimate how much difference it can make to the users of a wide range of services when they encounter someone who can use counselling skills effectively in their work. To enable workers to develop and use these skills appropriately, trainers need to adapt materials. If case materials and role plays are so removed from workers' own experience that they do not recognise themselves or their clients, they may have difficulty in projecting themselves into the situations described. If the materials seem irrelevant, course members may also fail to transfer the skills which they are learning into their everyday work situations. If the investment in training is to bear fruit, course tutors must adapt materials to reflect the experience and concerns of course members and their clients.

The trainer may have either a homogeneous group, drawn from a single workplace or profession, or a mixed group in which a number of work settings are represented. Ideally, trainers will have talked with course members and their managers prior to the course in order to arrive at an understanding of the work in which course members are engaged and particularly of those aspects of the work in which counselling skills would be most useful. If it is impracticable to do this face to face, we have found that a telephone call to a few prospective course members is extremely useful in finding out the particular situations in which they see counselling skills as potentially helpful. This information can then be used to adapt material for the particular group right from the first session.

Homogeneous groups

Assuming a hospital context, the vignette of Fatima (below) deals with making an approach to someone who seems isolated or distressed:

FATIMA:

> Fatima was admitted to your ward two days ago. You have noticed that she looks drawn and red-eyed and you suspect that from time to time she has been weeping. She makes only monosyllabic replies when addressed. As far as you know she has had no visitors. You have been very busy but you're feeling a little uncomfortable that you have not made time for her. You'd like to try and approach her...

An adaptation here is simply a matter of changing two sentences. The phrases which make this case study specific to a hospital setting are: 'Fatima was admitted to your ward...' and 'She has had no visitors.' By changing these phrases, the basic vignette can then be adapted as follows:

For an educational context:

A. 'Fatima joined your class... she has not made any friends in the group.'

For a workplace context:

B. 'Fatima started work in your office... she has not made any friends among her colleagues.'

For a playgroup:

C. 'Fatima brought her child to your playgroup... she has not made any friends among the other parents.'

For a drop-in centre:

D. 'Fatima came to your drop-in centre... she has not made any friends among the other users.'

The tutor can also add to the material (bearing in mind the training objectives), in order to fill out the situation a little.

For example, adding to B, C and D:

> 'She has not made any friends . . . , seeming to shrink into herself when others approach her.'

Having adapted materials for a so-called 'homogeneous group' there are, of course, always differences which emerge between course members' real work situations. For example, 'nurses' may work on children's or adult wards or in the community. A health visitor on a course which assumes that all nurses work on a hospital ward is likely to feel that his concerns are not being addressed. As a result, he may feel alienated from the course and, more importantly, may fail to make the link between practising skills on the course and using them in his everyday work.

Heterogeneous groups

When working with a heterogeneous group, it is important to include, over the period of the course, case studies to which all course members relate. Additionally, it may be possible to frame case studies in such a way as to enable all course members to 'read in' their own situations:

> You have been very busy recently but you have noticed that Fatima, who is a new arrival, looks drawn and red-eyed. You suspect that from time to time she has been weeping. She seems to shrink into herself when anyone approaches her and makes only monosyllabic replies when addressed. This has been going on for a couple of days now and you are feeling rather uncomfortable that you have not yet made time for her. You would like to try and approach her . . .

In early stages of training there may be value in grouping course members according to their place of work and using context-relevant materials (for example A above, for those in education, and so on). However, as course members become more confident and, particularly when they begin to recognise the value of learning from others in other contexts, they can work with and value the potential of the more generalised material.

Counselling skills in organisations

The fact that many more people are helped by those who use counselling skills (in roles such as nurse, youth worker, teacher, advice worker and so on) is sometimes disguised by the greater status accorded to private, one-to-one counselling by counselling skills course members. It is, therefore, easy for course tutors, unwittingly, to collude with this by using case materials in which it is assumed that the helper has unlimited time and an ever-available private place to meet. For many people, such situations have to be created among the demands of a busy day, often depending upon the goodwill of colleagues. If 'real-life' constraints such as these are not recognised and tackled in the training situation, course members and their future clients will be ill-served. This involves the use of case materials and role play in two respects: first, in ensuring that the material acknowledges the work situation of course members and, second, in using materials designed for the specific objective of enabling course members to manage the constraints of their own workplace. In effect, such skills as those involved in telling someone that you cannot give them time immediately, in making a sensitive referral and in negotiating authoritatively with colleagues and managers are fundamental. One role play which we have found very productive entails course members practising explaining to colleagues or prospective clients what counselling *is*.

As a further example, on a counselling skills course for those with a management responsibility, the following case study would allow them to discuss some of the constraints of their role and how they might deal with them:

> You are Henry's line manager and two days ago you had to tell him that he is to be made redundant in ten weeks' time. He did not seem to have much of a reaction then, but today he comes into your office and you can see he is quite anxious. You are due at a meeting, which you are chairing, in ten minutes and you are pretty sure that Henry needs more than ten minutes ...

For a personnel or welfare officer:

> You have offered Henry some time to talk through his feelings about the redundancy. He seems to want this, but has said he would be embarrassed to be seen in your office. You now have to tackle your manager about seeing Henry off-site.

Many course members on Diploma level courses will at some point in the future become specialist counsellors in organisations. The main business of the organisation is unlikely to be counselling or therapy (counsellors are now being employed in banks and other commercial enterprises as well as in health, education and social services). They may be the only trained counsellor, expected to take a wide range of referrals and to advise the whole organisation on matters within their range of expertise.

As trainers, we need to be aware of the full spectrum of skills which course members will need to be effective practitioners. This will involve their interactions with clients and potential clients, with colleagues and with the organisation as a whole. It will entail explaining what counselling is and what it can and cannot do; it will entail making decisions about who they should and should not work with; it will entail communicating boundaries such as confidentiality; it will entail supporting and advising colleagues; and it may well entail suggesting policy and procedural changes in order to assist the functioning of the organisation as a whole.

All these situations require course members to use their skills assertively. Case studies and role plays are invaluable in helping course members to find their authority and use it appropriately in their own work.

EQUAL OPPORTUNITIES OR DIFFERENCE AND DISCRIMINATION

We described on pages 12–13 how unrecognised assumptions can lead to discrimination against course members and their potential clients. There are a number of ways in which implicit assumptions can be conveyed through case study and role play materials. For example, the names used might communicate that the trainers assume all helpers to be of white, Anglo-Saxon origin. The context in which words like 'family' and 'relationship' are used might communicate the assumption that all partnerships are heterosexual. Where materials do deal with black or disabled people, they might only do so in ways which indicate that their race or disability is a 'problem'.

To take the case of 'Henry' as an example, the trainer might well think that making Henry overtly black, or disabled, or gay (he may, of course, be any or all of these) at an early stage could confuse and complicate the discussion on loss, thinking that course members could be sidetracked into a discussion on racism or sexual orientation. The question to ask, though, is *when* rather than *whether* to introduce such material and promote discussion. Black or gay or disabled course members themselves will certainly have experienced loss, and all course members are likely at some stage to work with black, disabled or gay clients who are experiencing loss. The reality of difference will have to be recognised at every stage. As with the other adaptations described above, the trainer's task is to make a professional judgement about the level of complexity appropriate to the group's development.

In practice, in many groups some or all of these issues will be raised by course members themselves. However, it is important that they feel facilitated rather than blocked by course tutors. According course members, from whatever background and experience, equal respect and value involves signalling respect and recognition for members of their community through the materials used. This makes it more likely that course members will enrich the learning of the whole group by contributing their own experiences of discrimination and oppression.

In terms of the course structure, we would strongly recommend that it is sufficiently flexible to allow for such sensitive issues to be raised and dealt with when they flow organically from the materials used. In this way, recognising and responding to experiences of discrimination become part of the day-to-day business, and learning from timetabled sessions such as 'Cross-Cultural Counselling' or 'Sexuality and Sexual Orientation' can be reinforced.

CONCLUSION

In this chapter we have shown how the 'items of information' in case and role play material can be adapted for use on different training courses and how key questions can be used with the same material to meet different objectives. In selecting and adapting materials, it is also important that trainers take into account:

- The different contexts in which course members will be using their skills.

- The range of clients they will be dealing with. (This includes factors such as age, gender, race, creed, sexual orientation and disablement.)

- The organisational and managerial constraints within which they will be working.

Part II contains a range of material, some of which will apply to your course members as it stands. We hope that, with the kinds of adaptation we have described, you will find most of it useful.

PART II
The resources

HOW TO USE PART II

We hope that the materials in Part II will spark off your creativity and help you speedily to generate effective and relevant teaching materials.

In Part I we talked about the need to identify clear training objectives, to select materials in order to meet those objectives and to adapt those materials to reflect the composition and circumstances of the training group. Part II contains a range of material which can be simplified, expanded and adapted according to the learning needs of your own group. Unlike Part I, to which normal copyright applies, the resources in Part II may be used and duplicated, provided that the source is acknowledged.

SELECTING MATERIALS

For practical purposes, we divide human experience into categories although ultimately it is indivisible; so we have made certain arbitrary decisions in structuring this material.

Part II is divided into two sections. Section A, 'Core Relationship Skills', covers the range of skills and considerations which lead to basic good practice, including the core conditions of counselling, beginnings and endings and ethical issues. Section B, 'Practice Themes', covers areas of concern which commonly emerge in the helping relationship. These include loss, bereavement, sexuality, race and culture, anxiety and so on.

The Materials Reference Table which follows shows how the sections are structured. Each group of materials is given a letter and a number (e.g. **A1**) relating it to a core relationship skill or basic practice theme, in this case the development of empathy. A second number identifies it specifically, e.g. **A1.4**, which is in fact the vignette of Duncan. Duncan is, or more correctly was, one of a couple who split up with his partner, David, and is still grieving the loss of that relationship. In addition to its use for developing empathy, the vignette can be used to understand more about intimate couple relationships and the feelings evoked by the loss of such a relationship.

This example illustrates how most of the materials have more than one application and throughout Part II we use these reference numbers to draw the reader's attention to related material. You will find in the section on gay and lesbian bereavement (**B2.9–12**) a reference to **A1.4** and if you are looking for general materials on gay and lesbian relationships, **A1.4** appears under the relevant heading in the Materials Reference Table: 'Categories across Sections A and B: Couples: Gays and Lesbians'.

To take another example: suppose you are planning a session on ethical counselling practice for people working in health care contexts. The Materials Reference Table tells you that Section **A4** refers to Ethics and Good Practice and that within this section there are materials relating to Referrals, Boundaries and Boundary Breaks. Looking under Health Contexts in 'Categories across Sections A and B' you will find that **A4.5**, **A4.15**, **A4.22**, **A4.34**, **A4.35** and **A4.48** are all 'ready-made' for health care workers.

THE FORM OF THE MATERIALS

Any of the resource materials can be used as the basis for discussion, or role play, or both; they are here in the form in which we last used them. This means that the 'voice' varies and might be that of the client or that of a third person describing the client. The categorisation described below may be obvious to an experienced trainer but may help to make sense of the Table on page 80 which summarises the forms in which the materials are presented.

The most common form is when the reader is put into the role of counsellor or helper and the material describes what the counsellor sees of the client's world, for example (**A3.1**):

> You are a helper at a centre for disabled children. Seamus's mother, Mrs S., . . . appears uncharacteristically dishevelled. You want to be understanding and when you reach out to her, tears come to Mrs S.'s eyes.

This we have called the *base form*. It invites the course member to imagine himself within a helping or counselling relationship and enables him to consider not only the client information but also his own inner responses and the constraints and possibilities of his own workplace.

Some vignettes simply describe the client, as in **A1.18**, Mr Barnes-Walker:

> Mr Barnes-Walker is a very correct, polite man who has recently retired from the armed forces. His wife died . . .

In such a case, a specific helper or counsellor role can be added to suit the course membership, for example:

He comes to your Social Services area office offering to do volunteer work with 'young lads who have gone astray'.

or

He comes to your surgery complaining of a stiffness in his neck and jaw, but you can find no physical cause.

Base form materials are easy to convert to role play instructions by separating out the elements of the counsellor from the client information and turning them into the 'you' form, for example:

Mr Barnes-Walker (client role)
You are a correct, polite man who has recently retired from the armed forces. Your wife died . . .

Dr Smith (listener role)
Your patient, Mr Barnes-Walker, is complaining of a stiffness in his neck and jaw, but you can find no physical cause. He has mentioned that his wife died a little while ago and you decide to ask him more . . .

Materials which are already in this form, with or without a specific listener or counsellor role, are designated as *role play* in the text. They can equally easily be converted to the *base form* if the preferred training method is discussion.

Sometimes several role plays are presented together as part of a family or other group. Trainers can use some or all of these in a *linked role play* or select just one of them, according to their training objectives.

Occasionally, the material is presented simply as the direct speech of the client: **A1.4**, for example:

'I'm feeling very low at the moment. Since David and I split up, I've been finding it very difficult . . .'

Presenting material in this form can enable course members to identify with and explore the meanings, tones and emphases of the client role as they 'say it in their heads'. Group discussion often brings out the importance of body language, tone of voice and facial expression to the listener's understanding.

Horseshoe role play also uses the form of direct speech but as a starting point for a tutor role rather than a focus for discussion. The materials which are designated as *horseshoe role play* also include further information to help the tutor to develop the role.

The categorisation of the materials according to the forms in which they appear is summarised in the Table on page 80. This should enable busy tutors to see at a glance which forms are immediately available within each area. However, it is more than likely that tutors will need to make some amendments to tailor the materials to their particular group or to meet their own training objectives.

USING NAMES

As well as a letter and number, we have also given a name or names to all of the vignettes and roles for ease of identification and cross-referencing. In practice it is often better not to use names at all. If vignettes are simply labelled A, B, C … (or 1, 2, 3 …) course members often make assumptions, for example that the person described is male or female, old or young, or about their race or sexuality. This can give rise to lively debate: 'Of course it's a woman – a man wouldn't …'. If such stereotyping is not challenged by course members themselves, tutors can raise awareness and encourage exploration by means of supplementary questions such as:

> 'If this person were a wheelchair user, what would be going on in your mind?'

> 'You seem to have made the assumption that this person is a man, which is not unreasonable for our society. If she were a woman, what would be the differences?'

If the material requires a name, there are several British names which are commonly used for either sex, such as Chris, Alex and Les. Sikh names are not gender-specific but in most other cultures, the same name is rarely used for both men and women.

FOCUSING THE LEARNING

At the beginning of subsections, we give examples of questions which might be used to focus the thinking of course members in order to achieve the training objectives. It is often helpful to reproduce these key questions in the form of instructions to the group. For example:

> Read the following studies one by one and, without considering them in any depth, note any reactions in yourself which might limit your initial acceptance of and warmth towards the person.

In groups of three to five people, read the case vignettes below. For each one, discuss how, in listener role, you might reflect back the feelings of the person speaking. Choose one response for each vignette and write it down. These responses will be discussed in the larger group.

As described in Chapter 2, learning can be built upon and consolidated if four or five vignettes are used as a basis for discussion. In Appendix 2 are examples of typical case material handouts to show the 'end result' of selected materials combined with key questions.

MATERIALS REFERENCE TABLE

SECTION A   CORE RELATIONSHIP SKILLS

A1   Core conditions: the basis for trust   83–94
1–15   Empathy
16–24   Unconditional positive regard (acceptance)
25–31   Congruence

A2   Developing the relationship   95–102
1–3   Development of an informal relationship through using
         counselling skills
4–10   Challenge when using counselling skills
11–16   Challenge in a counselling relationship

A3   Beginnings and endings   103–17
Beginnings
1–5   When moving into using counselling skills from a different role
6–10   A first counselling session with someone self-referred
11–15   A session with someone referred from another person or agency
16–19   A 'first' session after a previous experience of counselling
20–25   A session after a difficult previous session

Endings
26–29   First-session endings
30–37   More difficult sessions
38–42   Ending counselling relationships
43–48   More difficult counselling relationship endings

Interruptions
49–52   To the counselling relationship

A4   Ethics and Good Practice   118–39
Referral
1–3   From a role using counselling skills
4–7   As a result of limitations in your own experience
8–11   As a result of inappropriate professional and personal relationships
12–14   As a result of limitation of time or work overload
15–18   As a result of limitations of a personal nature
19–24   To a more appropriate mode of working
25–29   Receiving referrals

Boundaries
30–37   Creating and maintaining the counselling relationship boundary
         with other professionals
38–42   Creating and maintaining the counselling relationship boundary
         with other people

Boundary breaks
43–48   Confidentiality
49–55   Money issues
56–59   Presents
60–63   Sexual

80

SECTION B   PRACTICE THEMES

B1 Loss (General)   142–7
  1–7   Loss of 'objects' (purse, job, body parts, home, culture, etc.)
  8–13   Loss of relationships

B2 Bereavement   148–58
  1–8   Individuals and families
  9–16   Bereavements which easily go 'unnoticed' or unrecognised

        a) 9–12   Gay and lesbian bereavement
        b) 13–15 Miscarriage, abortion, stillbirth
        c) 16   Multiple ungrieved losses

  For other materials covering loss and bereavement, see also:
  A1. 17, 18, **A2.** 3, **A3.** 11, 12, 25, 33, 39, 43, 44, 45, 48, 51, **A4.** 3, 8, 14, 16

B3 Change and transition   159–62
  1–5   Adolescence and leaving home
  6–10   Additions
  11–14 Changing patterns of health, ageing and employment

B4 Sexuality   163–8
  1–6   Discovering sexuality
  7–10   Sex and relationships
  11–14 Sexuality and abuse of power

  For other materials covering sexuality, see also:
  A1. 23, **A2.** 13, **A3.** 23, 24, 33, **B2.** 8

B5 Race and culture   169–70
  1–6

  For other materials covering race and culture, see also:
  A1. 19, 22, **A4.** 6, 44, **B1.** 7, **B4.** 4, 5

B6 Disability   171–2
  1–5

  For other materials covering disability, see also:
  A1. 6, 20, 25, **B1.** 2, **B7.** 4

B7 Stress, anxiety, depression   173–7
  1–11

  For other materials covering stress, anxiety and depression, see also:
  A1. 3, **A3.** 19, 44, 52, **A4.** 5, 17, 22

  For materials covering substance abuse, see: **A3.** 12, 15, 17, **A4.** 18, 28

CATEGORIES ACROSS SECTIONS A AND B

A large number of the materials in Part II can be used in any context and, as described in Chapter 5 of Part I, materials can often be easily adapted to different client groups and different contexts. The references below cover only those materials which make specific reference to the categories described.

Families

A1. 11, 13, 17, 19, 20, 23, **A2.** 2, 11, 16, **A3.** 1, 38, **A4.** 21, 32, 40, 45, **B1.** 5, 6, 10, 11, **B2.** 4, 5, 6, 7, 8, **B3.** 2, 3, 8, 9, **B4.** 10

Couples

A1. 4, 7, 15, **A2.** 3, 12, **A3.** 10, 27, 32, 48, **A4.** 3, 20, 22, 24, 38, **B1.** 9, 12, **B2.** 9, 10, 11, 12, **B3.** 4, 6, 7, 10, 13, 14, **B4.** 7, 8, 9, 12, **B7.** 5

Gays and lesbians: **A1.** 4, 23, **A4.** 22, 24, **B2.** 9, 10, 11, 12, **B4.** 2, 10, 14

Children and young people

A1. 2, 4, 5, 8, 14, 16, 17, 20, 25, 27, 30, **A2.** 6, 9, **A3.** 2, 4, 14, 38, **A4.** 6, 9, 12, 17, 21, 32, 40, 41, 43, 46, 54, **B3.** 1, 2, 3, 4, **B4.** 1, 2, 3, **B6.** 4, **B7.** 1, 7, 8

Older adults

A2. 5, **A3.** 11, 15, 24, **A4.** 10, 13, 16, 22, 50, 53, **B2.** 11, 16, **B3.** 11, 12, **B7.** 2

General work contexts

A1. 7, 8, 10, 13, 14, 26, **A2.** 1, 5, 8, 10, 14, **A3.** 30, 34, **A4.** 3, 8, 23, 30, 33, 37, 39, 44, **B4.** 11, **B5.** 2, 4, **B6.** 1, 2, **B7.** 3, 9

Health contexts

A1. 15, **A2.** 3, **A3.** 3, 5, 11, 19, **A4.** 5, 15, 22, 34, 35, 48, **B2.** 1, **B5.** 3, **B7.** 6

Pregnancy, miscarriage, stillbirth, abortion: **A1.** 16, **A3.** 13, 15, 45, **A4.** 35, 38, **B2.** 13, 14, 15

Social services contexts

A1. 23, **A2.** 9, **A3.** 1, 11, **A4.** 13, 17, 21, 36, 45, **B7.** 2

Educational contexts

A1. 2, 5, 16, 27, **A2.** 16, **A3.** 2, 6, 14, 16, 17, **A4.** 6, 9, 12, 32, 43, 60, **B6.** 3, 5, **B7.** 10

SECTION A: CORE RELATIONSHIP SKILLS MATERIAL

A1. CORE CONDITIONS: THE BASIS FOR TRUST

Empathy and acceptance (or unconditional positive regard) are the starting points and the bedrock of successful relationships. In the initial stages of training, the emphasis will be on raising course members' awareness of the extent and limitations of their own acceptance of themselves and others. The tutor's role is to demonstrate acceptance of course members – even though they may themselves be expressing judgements and prejudices in relation to the case study material and each other. Through the tutor's empathic rephrasing of reactions to the material, course members will begin to perceive their own and each others' underlying feelings and constructs.

Empathy

The first stage in developing empathy is to ask course members to focus on the feelings aroused by the case study, their own and others', and to alert them to the difference between feeling and thinking.

The second stage is to ask course members to formulate possible responses through group discussion. This gives them time to consider what they might actually say to someone and hear how it might be received by others.

The third stage is, through role play, to enable them to put this learning into practice so that they are 'thinking on their feet'. Course members may need time to appreciate that their perception of others' feelings, however clear in their own mind, does not automatically 'show' and that it is only through considerable practice in verbalising their perceptions that they will become skilled in empathic responding.

For stages one and two, it is often helpful to select five or six vignettes and to reproduce key questions in the form of instructions to the group.

Example instructions:

> *Read the case studies below. After you have read each one, note down the feelings which may be behind the statement.*

> *In groups of 3 to 5 people, read the case studies below. For each one, discuss how, in counsellor role, you might reflect back the feelings of the person speaking. Choose one response for each vignette and write down what you would say. These responses will be discussed in the larger group.*

A1. 1 *Chris*

'I've been out of work three years now and I'm just fed up of not having any money. All I want to do is work but no matter what I do, no one will give me a job. I've got to have *some* way of relaxing and even if I just go to see a friend it costs seventy pence on the bus. That's without going for a drink or anything.'

A1. 2 *Arabella*

'Mr Eliot is always picking on me. It's not fair. Other people talk and muck about but the minute I open my mouth he's on at me. It's his fault anyway. If his lessons weren't so boring I wouldn't want to talk, would I?'

A1. 3 *Sanjay*

'I just can't be bothered any more. I don't seem to be able to get going somehow. It's as if I'm looking at myself thinking, "It's about time you got off your backside and did some work." But I don't. Nothing seems that important, somehow' [eyes fill with tears].

A1. 4 *Duncan*

'I'm feeling very low at the moment. Since David and I split up, I've been finding it difficult to do any more than get myself to work and back. We were together for nine years and there are so many reminders.'

A1. 5 *Molly*

'I try to be nice to them but they still get at me. One of them hid my bag yesterday and they were all laughing. I hate them all. I wish I could ... oh I don't know. I just wish someone would pick on *them*. Then they'd know. And the teachers don't do anything. I hate them too.'

A1. 6 *Penelope*

'It's all Isabelle, Isabelle. "Isabelle doesn't moan. Isabelle is such a lovely girl." They just feel sorry for her because she can't walk. It's me who has to *do* everything. "Isabelle can't do the washing up. It's not her fault, is it?" If anyone tells me what a saint Isabelle is just one more time, I'll scream. They just *expect* me to do things. If I left home they'd only notice when they found the dirty dishes.'

A1. 7 *Denise and Jeremy*

A colleague of yours, Denise, comes into the room and you notice that she is rather tearful. You wonder what is wrong and she pours out her story about Jeremy, who she says has lately given in to rather frequent outbursts of temper. Denise has tried to calm the situation but it seems to keep ending up with Jeremy verbally attacking Denise who then wishes she had dealt better with the situation.

A1. 8 *Saul*
(Role Play)

You have been feeling much more confident as a result of taking part in an adult training scheme (you are 35). You are on work placement at the local supermarket. Your boss has told you that you are too 'slow' to be offered a job at the end of the scheme. You are very upset about this and you don't really know what he means. You've been very happy there and you thought you were doing all right. You always get there on time and you've only ever had two days off (because of 'flu). You found it difficult at first because you didn't always understand what people meant yet people seemed to want to help you. Now you're not really sure you can trust them any more.

A1. 9 *Ifeani*

You have known Ifeani for a few months. You like him and you feel you have built up a good relationship with him. You put a lot of work into finding him the opportunity for a job which would suit him and arranged an interview for him last week. He comes to tell you that he didn't turn up for the interview. He had another interview some months ago and through nervousness made a complete hash of it. He still feels embarrassed whenever he thinks of it. This time he got ready and went to the firm but couldn't face walking through the gates.

Note: Tutor may need to encourage the Careers Adviser, Personnel Officer or Employment Officer to recognise and manage their own frustration in order to recognise Ifeani's crippling anxiety.

A1. 10 *Appraiser and Appraisee*
(Role Play)

Appraiser

You have an appraisal session with a member of staff who is highly thought of by many colleagues, and competent in the technical and interpersonal aspects of the job. You will enjoy passing on all the favourable comments.

Appraisee

You have an appraisal session with one of your managers. You know that you are doing well generally and you get on well with colleagues. You are worried, though, that you are finding work on the new project more difficult. The supervisory manager expects you to do it all brilliantly and doesn't seem to listen when you ask for help. You don't know how to get the message across without showing yourself up in front of the others.

Note: Tutor may need to remind course members about the difference between empathy and reassurance and the importance of staying within the 'Appraisee's' frame of reference.

A1. 11 *Helga*

'I don't know what you think about it. Our Anna is really getting me down. The last thing I want is for her to grow up with the same problem as me. I've told her time and time again "You've got to stick at it my girl and not be as thick as your mother." But now the school's telling me she's behind with her reading. I said "That's it! No more 'Neighbours' till your teacher says you're getting somewhere."'

Note: remember that Helga is the client, not Anna.

A1. 12 *James*

'No, I don't want to read anything. I'm fed up with this fucking place anyway. I wouldn't be here if it wasn't for me social worker. He's bloody well at me all the time.'

A1. 13 *Diane*

'It's no good [starting to cry]. I just can't concentrate on anything. I don't think there's any point coming into work when I feel like this. I've got that many problems. I seem to be so angry and twisted up inside I can't think of anything except Bill and what he's doing to us all – sometimes I feel as if I'd like to murder him.'

Note: It may be more useful to focus on Diane's feelings rather than getting side-tracked into the confused context.

A1. 14 *Gasena*
(Role Play)
Some friends of yours are travelling to see a tourist show on its last day in this country. You desperately want to go but you know you can't afford to miss a day's work. Should you go sick for the day and risk not enjoying yourself because you know you're doing wrong or should you come clean and ask to make up the work – knowing you'll have burnt your boats if the response is unsympathetic?

A1. 15 *Nuala*
A young nurse, new to the ward, asks to have a word with you about one of the auxiliaries who has been at this hospital for over ten years. She tells you that the auxiliary refused to allow a diabetic patient any potato with her meal. The patient was very upset by this, pointing out that she had 'budgeted' her carbohydrate allowance to give herself the potato. The auxiliary, an overbearing woman, apparently simply refused to listen. The young nurse is clearly distressed about the incident. She says she has had difficulties before with the auxiliary but has backed down rather than have an argument within patients' hearing. She didn't know how to handle this one, so pretended not to hear and now feels dreadful.

Unconditional positive regard (acceptance)

There may be things about these clients which might make them difficult to accept. Learning and discovering which clients we find most difficult can be a way of discovering which aspects of ourselves we struggle to accept.

Example instructions:

> *Read the following studies one by one and, without considering them in any depth, note any reactions in yourself which might limit your initial acceptance of and warmth towards, that person.*

> *Read the case studies below one by one. For each one, without thinking deeply, give yourself a mark from one to five. One indicates that you feel very accepting of the person. Five indicates that you find yourself making a strong judgement. (Note that approval is just as much of a judgement as disapproval.)*

> *If you find yourself struggling to accept the person described, what are some of the things you might do about this?*

A1. 16 *Patty*

Patty is outgoing and sociable and you feel that she has a better chance than most of being offered work at the end of her course. You notice and say to her that today she looks tired and strained. She then tells you that her period is nearly a week overdue, which is very unusual for her. She's afraid she's pregnant. She then tells you that she has been going out with the same boy for about six months and is quite fond of him. They slept together three or four times over the past two months and Patty relied on him to know whether it was 'safe'. He knows about her fears and wants to marry her if she is pregnant. Her parents are Roman Catholic, although they don't always go to church. Patty thinks her mother might be sympathetic but she would not want to face her father. She is considering an abortion.

A1. 17 *Gary* (see **A3.** 42)

Gary has been made redundant and is desperate to get another job. He is pretending to his family that he still has work because he feels his wife has enough worries at the moment. He leaves home in the morning and returns in the evening as if he had been at work.

A1. 18 *Mr Barnes-Walker*

Mr Barnes-Walker is a very correct, polite man who has recently retired from the armed forces. His wife died six months ago, so he is looking for some occupation where he could be of use to the community. Perhaps helping to put young lads who have gone astray back on the 'straight and narrow'.

A1. 19 *Leroy*

Leroy's parents emigrated from Jamaica to England when he was a youngster, to make a better life for the family. Leroy was left in the care of his grandmother. He is feeling very bitter towards his parents for first leaving him and then bringing him away from his grandmother. He has cut himself off from his parents and never wants to see them again.

A1. 20 *Ben*

Ben is a young man with a learning disability who is having difficulties in his relationship with his parents, feeling that they don't give him any freedom and treat him like a child. His clothes are extremely dirty and he continually wipes his runny nose on his sleeve.

A1. 21 *Jenny*

Jenny is a deeply religious woman for whom God is a constant companion and the inspiration for her life. She cares uncomplainingly for her disabled husband and her three young grandchildren while her own children work. When she feels weary and when her back hurts, as it often does, she counts her blessings and berates herself for 'sinful thoughts'. 'You must accept suffering in this life', she tells you, 'in preparation for the next'.

A1. 22 *Rifat*

Rifat's forthcoming marriage has been arranged by her parents. She is very angry at the sympathy expressed by her white colleagues, pointing out that arranged marriages are at least as successful as so-called 'love matches'. She is proud of her cultural heritage and criticises the way youngsters are brought up in white English families.

A1. 23 *Hazel*

Hazel has been married for twelve years and has three children. She has been struggling since her teenage years to fulfil her family's expectations but has recently fallen in love and begun a lesbian relationship. She intends to 'come out' to her family and friends.

Note: Daljit (below) could be used as part of the case studies series for testing acceptance. However, his case is also very useful as a Horseshoe role play to give course members the opportunity to practise responding to someone whose attitudes may be difficult for them to accept.

A1. 24 *Daljit*
(Horseshoe Role Play)

Daljit (played by tutor)

> 'I want some proper advice from you. I've been to see the Citizens' Advice people, the Welfare Rights people and I don't know who else, but nobody is any help. They only tell me I have to budget properly. What with? You've got to have money to budget with and I haven't got any. I don't see why I shouldn't have a drink with the lads or a car or a telly like everyone else. It isn't my fault I can't get a job.'

Note: The tutor might become increasingly angry, since course members may find it difficult to respond in an accepting way to someone who seems to be angry with them.

Congruence

Congruence is only effective within a relationship demonstrating empathy and acceptance. The case studies below offer the opportunity to discuss the effects of using or not using congruent responses in a number of situations. Prior to the discussion, course members will need help with understanding the difference between owning and expressing their own thoughts and feelings and less helpful behaviours such as blaming and projecting. Role playing the situations then gives them the opportunity to practise skills.

Example key questions:

> *Read the case studies below and, for each one, discuss your own reactions to the person speaking. Would your reaction help or hinder your ability to listen to this person?*

> *Note the feelings evoked in you by these case studies. Spend a few minutes thinking about your own feelings and making sure you recognise them as your own.*

> *In pairs (or groups) begin to think about how you could congruently express your reaction to each of the people in the studies below. Then discuss whether or not your congruence could be helpful and how it might help.*

A1. 25 *Travis*

Tracy is 17 and has learning difficulties. She is a large, well-developed girl but with a very unsophisticated appearance, wearing drab clothes and with her hair in 'bunches'. She is always affectionate, especially with male members of staff, clinging to them and rubbing herself against them. Attempts have been made to discourage this. Your male colleague, Travis, comes to you at break for some help. He says that Tracy followed him into the stock cupboard, grabbed his hand and put it down the front of her blouse. He feels totally at a loss and suggests you might 'do some sex education with her'.

A1. 26 *Justin*

Justin, a colleague at your workplace, asks, very nervously, if he could have counselling sessions. Before you can answer he demands to know whether you are a Rogerian, Gestalt, Psychodynamic or Transactional Analysis Counsellor, as he says he knows something about therapy.

A1. 27 *John*

John has an important exam at the end of the year. He says he cannot afford to fail it but is neglecting the work because he is having difficulties in a relationship which is also important to him. He agrees he is not doing any work for the exam but feels sure that he will be able to catch up. As the exam approaches, you become sure that he is kidding himself and is in serious danger of blowing his chances.

A1. 28 *Chris*

'Do you know, I always feel better for having talked to you. It's as though you understand everything before I even say it. You are on the same wavelength as me. You are the only person I ever talk to like this. That's because I trust you not to laugh at me or tell me to shut up. You really are very good at what you do. I'd actually like to see you more often, because in between times it's awful. No one else understands what's going on for me. I think that if I saw you once or twice a week, I'd soon get myself sorted out – you're so good at counselling people. Or could I perhaps have your 'phone number – just for an emergency?'

Note: This also works well as a Horseshoe role play, with the tutor playing the role. The tutor might become increasingly sweet and sugary as course members often find it difficult to confront that kind of 'sweetness'.

A1. 29 *Naomi* (see **A3.** 45)

You have met Naomi twice now, to help her with difficult work relationships. She is very articulate, very clear about what is going wrong and very specific in outlining her various courses of action – resignation, confrontation, formal complaint and so on. Her story is very factual, highly detailed and stark in its lack of emotional content. When you try to empathise with what seem to you to be underlying feelings of hurt, rejection, loneliness and confusion, she denies feeling anything.

A1. 30 *Dean*

Dean is a lively, engaging lad who is constantly in trouble. Things are always going wrong for him: equipment breaks, he misses his appointments with you, he loses things, fights break out in his wake. None of this is ever his fault. 'I was just holding it and it fell apart', 'I thought it was next week', 'I don't know why they were fighting – I didn't say that much.'

A1. 31 *Rehka* (see **A3.** 41)

Rehka has considerable difficulties with her family and the expectations they have of her. You reflect her frustration and impatience to her, but she rejects your empathy with a succession of 'yes but...'s. Although she seems genuinely to want things to change, none of the options she has explored with you so far has been acceptable to her and neither do her own feelings seem to be acceptable to her. You are finding it increasingly difficult to offer anything to her.

A2. DEVELOPING THE RELATIONSHIP

Development of a relationship through using counselling skills

Each of the following case studies demonstrates the possible effect of using counselling skills over time. Course members should have available to them the theoretical framework on which the course is based so that they can understand the change process as explained by the theory. After the changes have been understood, the tutor can lead a discussion on possible ways forward: continue with counselling skills; make a referral; move to a counselling contract and so on.

One way of using the case study chosen is to separate the case into three consecutive stages to be given to course members one at a time, asking them key questions as a prompt for discussion at each stage. For example:

Key questions for Stage 1

> *What is your initial response to this person?*
> *What might this person be feeling?*
> *How might you reflect back or check out content and feelings?*
> *(Try out some phrases and see how they sound.)*

Key questions for Stage 2

> *How has your relationship with this person progressed since the first meeting?*
> *What are the feelings and how might you reflect them?*
> *How would you respond?*

Key questions for Stage 3

> *Looking at all three extracts, can you explain, with reference to theory X, what changes are happening?*
> *How would you want to proceed with this person?*

A2. 1 *Len*

Len works in your organisation but not in your department. Whenever his name is mentioned, there are groans from colleagues. He buttonholes anyone he can and talks at great length. It has got to the point when most people avoid him. You believe that he might be quite hurt about the way he is treated and decide to listen to him properly instead of just dismissing him as a pain in the neck. Len comes to sit with you in the coffee bar and, as usual, starts to talk:

> What's the point in bothering. I'm never going to get a decent job. No one wants to know. It's because I don't suck up to them like other people. I've been doing this for nearly ten years now and I've virtually taught half the people here their jobs. But you never get any thanks, do you. They're even trying to move me downstairs. I know who's behind it. Millicent. She's never liked me because I say what I think and now the others can't be seen talking to me or she'll do the same to them. Silly sods. Like a load of sheep. Keep in with the right people and you'll get on. Huh. They'll learn.

You try to show acceptance through empathic reflecting, as you do the next two or three times you see Len. You find it harder work than you expected and you suspect that your own impatience shows at times. However, as you go on, you find that Len is beginning to talk more about himself:

> I wish I could keep my mouth shut sometimes. I can see straight away I've put people's backs up. I just get so wound up. I used to have lots of friends here and now they've all gone. I don't think this lot like me very much, really. I don't know why. I try to help when people first come – look after them a bit, you know – show them the ropes. Perhaps I do it wrong. Oh well, I don't know why I'm bothering about them. It's not worth it, is it?

After about the fifth or sixth informal meeting, you are beginning to understand how lonely Len is feeling and start to think that he needs more time and skill than you can give. Although he seems not to bother about talking so intimately in the coffee bar, you are uncomfortable at what other people might overhear – like when he said:

> I feel a bit stupid talking to you like this but I keep thinking about it all. I think the reason I don't get on with people is that I never know what to say, really. I just come out with stupid things as if I know it all. But I don't. It's always been like that. Do you think I say stupid things?

A2. 2 *Jasmine*

You are in the middle of preparing for a meeting which is due to start in ten minutes. You can hear a raised voice. It is Jasmine, whom you have met once before, sounding very agitated and insisting on seeing someone. Your phone rings and you are asked to deal with the situation. You say to Jasmine, 'It sounds as if you have something pretty important to talk about and I'm due at a meeting in ten minutes. How about us meeting afterwards, at one o'clock? Then I'll have a good three quarters of an hour and I can concentrate on you instead of worrying about my meeting.' Jasmine is inclined to be stroppy, but you are pleasant and firm and she agrees to come back. When you are both settled in a private room, she bursts out:

> Tell me how I can put my kids in care. I hate them. They're always doing things they shouldn't. Hitting them doesn't make any difference. Locking them up in their rooms doesn't make any difference. They just cheek me all the time. They nick money from me and Tony – and he says he's going to leave me if I can't control them better. Well I can't, so they'll just have to go.

At the end of this meeting, you say to her, 'You seem to be feeling at the end of your tether at the moment. Perhaps you need someone to listen to *you* for a bit. I haven't got any more time at the moment but we could meet for an hour next Tuesday morning – or Friday at about eleven – if you want to?' Jasmine takes you up on the offer.

During the second session, she says:

> I just can't cope any more. I couldn't bear to be on my own. I sometimes wish that Tony would do more with the kids but he just doesn't want to know. All he does is order them around, which works when he's there but he's never in nowadays. He always said he was no good with kids, but I thought it'd change when he had his own.
>
> I wanted kids so much. I was going to be completely different from my Mum – not hit them, not shout at them. But I'm useless as a mother. I get wound up and just scream at them. They'd be much better off without me.

You agree to see Jasmine again, and at one point during the third session she says:

> I feel so lonely sometimes. [Starts to become tearful.] I'm sure Tony's going to leave me sooner or later. I've tried so hard to keep the family together. I'm just useless. No good to anyone. My Mum always said that. *She* knew I'd make a mess of things. [Starts weeping.]

You are beginning to worry about the amount of time you can give her and about your own level of skill to help her, and think it might be appropriate to refer her for further help.

Note: For referral skills see Section **A4**.

A2. 3 *Hamutal and Michael*

You are a nurse on a cancer ward. Hamutal is in her thirties. She had one ovary removed two years ago and now she is in again for an extended examination and the possible removal of her other ovary and, possibly, uterus. Her partner, Michael, always seems to be on the ward, yet he talks to nobody – hardly even to Hamutal.

One evening, you find Michael alone and silent in the coffee room and decide to approach him. You sit down beside him and say that you imagine he's probably feeling pretty anxious about what is happening to Hamutal. At first he looks extremely wary, but when he realises that you are not going to blame him for anything he begins, haltingly at first, to talk about his fears and confusion:

> The worst thing is wondering what's going to happen to her. I wish all the tests were finished. I know she's going to be all right really, but you do just wonder, sometimes. It's hard going back to an empty house. I suppose people are getting fed up of me hanging around.

After a while he looks tired and you are expected back on the ward, so you finish off and invite him to approach you again if he wants to talk.

A few days later, Hamutal asks if you would have a word with Michael. When you look puzzled, she goes on to say that 'He needs to talk with someone and you are the only one he trusts.' When you find an opportunity to approach Michael, he says, 'I feel bad about using up your time like this. I know I shouldn't have to, really.' You empathise with his difficulty in talking, realising that his protests may cover some strong feelings which he cannot yet express. Eventually, he tells you that his mother died from cancer two years earlier. Supported by your acceptance and empathy, he manages to tell you how guilty he still feels about not doing enough for her.

The next day, he seeks you out. He has begun to realise that his feelings around his mother's death are getting in the way of his being close to Hamutal at the moment 'when she needs me most'. He wants you to help him be more 'present' with Hamutal.

Note: The tutor may wish to raise the possibility that Michael's guilt is spilling over into his relationship with Hamutal or that he has painful feelings about the children he may never have.

Challenge when using counselling skills

Before using case study and role play material to practise challenge or confrontation, it is important to explain their place within an empathic relationship. Course members also need to understand that empathy, unconditional positive regard and congruence can all be challenging, depending on the client's self-concept and self-perception and that the helper or counsellor cannot always predict what a client will find challenging.

The materials below include some instances where counselling challenge may be appropriate and others where it may not.

*The first set, **A2.** 4–10, indicates instances in a counselling skills context, the second set, **A2.** 11–17, includes instances from a counselling relationship.*

A2. 4 *Frank*
(Role Play)

Work has been extremely busy all day. You notice that one of your colleagues in particular is out of sorts and is not coping as well as he usually does. You are taken aback, however, when he comes to you to tell you he is handing in his notice since you think that he is pretty good at his job.

A2. 5 *Mrs Bailey*
Mrs Bailey lost her husband six months ago and cannot stop thinking about him. She says she realises she should have got over it by now and she has come because her children have told her she must get out and meet new people. She is very anxious to please and agrees with everything you say.

A2. 6 *Tommy*
At the youth club you have been working with Tommy, who first came to you when he needed help to stay off drugs. This week Tommy seems to be very distant. In the coffee bar, by chance, you get the opportunity to ask how he is getting on. He replies: 'Just great.'

A2. 7 *Ena*
Ena, a member of your group has recently failed to get a job you know she desperately wanted. When you ask how she is feeling about it, she replies nonchalantly: 'I didn't want it anyway.'

A2. 8 *Fred*
A colleague, Fred, keeps saying that he knows he ought to go on a diet and get fit. Then he says with a defeated air that he can't afford an exercise bicycle yet.

A2. 9 *Peter*
Peter is in care but sees his parents occasionally. He is always complaining that no one really 'cares', and is adamant about joining the fishing fleet as a junior trawlerman like his father did as a young man. Peter however, is only five feet tall, of slight build and has never been on a boat.

A2. 10 *Pat*
A member of staff, Pat, says to you: 'A lot of people are annoyed by the way management handled the changeover.'

Challenge in a counselling relationship

A2. 11 *Fanny*

The person you have been working with has been having a difficult time with her mother and after complaining bitterly to you, says: 'I do my best but it's her fault that we don't get on.'

A2. 12 *Elza and Joe*

You have been working with Elza and Joe for four weeks. Joe is bright and lively and seems used to getting his own way. Elza is much more subdued and has said a couple of times: 'I don't know what I want. I don't think it matters anyway.'

A2. 13 *Eve*

You have been working as a counsellor with a woman client for six weeks. She now discloses to you that she had a sexual relationship with her previous counsellor. She says that he asked her a number of times whether she really wanted this and she said yes. She says that she found him very attractive and feels responsible for the *affaire*. It was short-lived, however, because he became worried about his reputation. Now she feels hopeless because she has lost everything – again. Even her belief that she can be counselled. She always makes a mess of everything.

A2. 14 *Jo*

'There's no point in bothering any more. It's worse than last week. The place is so disorganised you can't get anything done. Management hasn't a clue what's really happening and they don't listen when you try to tell them.'

A2. 15 *Martha*

'It happened again. I came home and the dishes were still in the sink and he was sitting there watching the telly. I was so furious. I stood there doing the dishes and he didn't take a blind bit of notice.'

A2. 16 *Charlie and his mother*

You are in the Open Learning workshop when Charlie's mother comes in, followed by a rather reluctant Charlie, and says, 'There you are – I keep telling him he can't get himself to the bus on time in the mornings.' In further conversation, she says Charlie has always been delicate, she thinks he is being over-ambitious and his father is always saying he'd be better off on one of those special YTS schemes doing practical things.

You know Charlie as a quiet and studious student who has an exceptional talent for Art. He is anxious to get GCSE qualifications and go on to a BTEC course on the other side of the city. He is 17 and has severe hearing loss.

A2. 17 *Les*

(Horseshoe Role Play)

The task of the tutor is to witter on about everyday events. S/he should only move on to underlying concerns in response to appropriate challenge from course members.

> Well, as I was saying last week, my uncle and aunt visited yesterday. They're very nice people really, although I'm usually glad when they go. They've got three children and Jenny, who's the youngest, left home last year so they bought a dog . . .

A3. BEGINNINGS AND ENDINGS

Beginnings

In all beginnings, it is important to establish the working basis right from the start. This is true whether a practitioner is moving to use counselling skills from another role, beginning a counselling relationship or beginning a session. Sometimes this is quite straightforward, with boundaries such as those of time, place, role and, possibly, payment already clear. At other times, there may be complexities such as a mismatch of expectation or misunderstanding to do with task or role.

Beginnings: When moving into using counselling skills from a different role

A3. 1 *Mrs S.* (also **A3.** 26)

You are a helper at a home for physically disabled children. Seamus's mother, Mrs S., is usually very organised and extremely well dressed. She normally bakes a special cake for Seamus on a Saturday. Today she arrives without the cake and appears uncharacteristically dishevelled. You want to be understanding and when you reach out to comfort her, tears come to Mrs S.'s eyes. You think it might be helpful to let her talk about her feelings.

A3. 2 *Miranda* (also **A3.** 27)

You are Miranda's A Level English teacher as well as her personal tutor. You know that Miranda's parents have recently separated and are aware of Miranda as stiff and 'buttoned-up' at the moment. Towards the end of a discussion in the English class (about Casaubon's misunderstanding of Dorothea in Middlemarch and the ways in which men can still misunderstand women) you notice Miranda trying to fight off tears. As this is the last class of the day you decide to offer Miranda half an hour or so to 'offload'.

A3. 3 *Colin* (see **A3.**35)

Colin is a passionate footballer who was knocked off his bicycle two days ago by a drunken driver and suffered multiple fractures to his left leg. You are staff nurse on the orthopaedic ward where Colin is still bed-bound. You were slightly shocked to see Colin tip his whole food tray on to the floor. You decide to try and get a sense of Colin's feelings (so ask an orderly to clear up the mess) and approach the other side of Colin's bed yourself.

A3. 4 *Billy*

You are a youth worker who, after a particularly successful and exhilarating drama session with the youth group, is closing up the centre now that everyone has left, or so you thought. You notice that what looked like a pile of old coats is actually Billy curled up and (apparently) totally withdrawn. You remember that he hasn't really taken part this evening and you decide to try and understand what is happening for him.

A3. 5 *Greg* (also **A3.** 28)

You are a GP and your patient, Greg, has recently agreed to a course of mild steroid treatment for an otherwise untreatable condition. You have asked him to report back after ten days of treatment and he appears as arranged. When you ask about the treatment he throws the tablets on to the desk with his left hand and starts 'drumming' on the desk with his right. Knowing that he is the last patient that evening you decide to approach his state of mind rather than focus on his physical condition.

Beginnings: A first counselling session with someone self-referred

The tutor can encourage exploration by the counsellor of any prejudgements or misperceptions the client may be bringing to the counselling. For instance, the client may be tempted to make social remarks and so on, not really understanding the nature of counselling.

A3. 6 *Leon* (see **A3.** 31)

Leon has a reputation for very high academic achievement and has recently joined the teaching staff of your institution. You know that he recently stormed out of a departmental meeting and subsequently cancelled his classes for two days. He turns up at your office asking whether he can talk to you in total confidence.

A3. 7 *Manu*

Manu has made an appointment to see you and arrives wearing what look like three coats on a mild spring afternoon.

A3. 8 *Arabella* (also **A3.** 29)

Arabella has as far as you know sought your help from her own free will. When she comes in, however, before you've even said 'Hello', she bursts out with 'How can counselling be of any help?'

A3. 9 *Malawa*

Malawa made her appointment to see you several weeks ago. She comes in, stares at you with large eyes, blinks, turns away shyly, and looks down. She says nothing, but then looks at you from under her long eyelashes . . .

A3. 10 *Tony and Bob*

Bob and Tony arrive in your office. You know nothing about them except that the receptionist said they 'wanted to talk to someone'.

Beginnings: a session with someone referred from another person or agency

The tutor should stress to counsellors the importance of recognising the referral source and possible misunderstandings about counselling in the client as well as possible ambivalent feelings about starting with someone new. This section has similarities with the section on Receiving referrals (**A4.** 25–29) on p. 127.

A3. 11 *Mrs B.*

You work in a home for the elderly and you notice that Mrs B. has been losing weight recently. You ask the GP on her next visit to give Mrs B. a physical check-up. She finds nothing physically wrong and tells you she has encouraged Mrs B. to talk to you about any worries she may have. You remember then that Mrs B.'s daughter has recently left for a month to stay with her brother in Australia and it will soon be the anniversary of Mr B.'s death. You want to make it easy for Mrs B. to talk ...

A3. 12 *Peter*

Peter has been referred by his priest to the local drop-in centre where you work as a volunteer. There is a professional counsellor available but at present she has a full case load. Peter prefers to talk to a volunteer who is attending a counselling skills course rather than have no support while he is on the waiting list. During your first session, Peter reveals that he lost his job ten years ago because of redundancy. Subsequently his wife left him, taking their two children with her. He had to sell his house as a result of the divorce settlement. He is now in temporary accommodation and has been drinking heavily for some years.

Note: The counsellor might need time to consider the options available and the feelings that might arise for both Peter and the volunteer, before thinking about responding.

A3. 13 *Sharon*

You are a counsellor at a local pregnancy advisory service. Sharon is a single high-flyer with a lot of responsibility in her prestigious job. She has already had two terminations of pregnancy and when her male GP tells her that she is pregnant for the third time she suddenly wants to talk to somebody, but not to her GP. She says she would rather talk to a woman and he refers her to you at the service.

A3. 14 *Anne-Marie*

You are a school counsellor. Anne-Marie was caught up in a fight next to the school gates at the lunch-hour. The caretakers on lunch duty were surprised to find Anne-Marie in a fight and encouraged her to go along and talk to you. She comes in dishevelled and in tears . . .

A3. 15 *Mr O.* (see **A4.** 19)

You do some voluntary counselling for a local Church Counselling Service. The vicar had noticed that Mr and Mrs O. didn't seem to come to church together these days. When, one evening after choir practice, he saw Mr O. sort of 'hovering' as if to talk to him, he went over and asked Mr O. how Mrs O. was. Initially he received only a mumbled kind of response, but Mr O. then managed to say that things were 'not too good'. Since their daughter's second miscarriage, Mrs O. had been drinking more and more and Mr O. simply didn't know how to address the drinking. Nor was he able to talk about his own feelings. The vicar then encouraged him to contact a local Church Counselling Service.

Beginnings: A 'first' session after a previous experience of counselling

Tutors would need to highlight the importance of re-contracting and exploring anything 'left over' from the previous contact, whether with you or with someone else. Strong negatives or positives might need to be understood in the context of the client's internal world.

A3. 16 *Teresa*

Teresa is now in her third year at college. She had seen you for twenty sessions in her first year when troubles in her own country had made it particularly difficult for her to settle in (at college). As far as you know the troubles in her own country have settled down, since her country is no longer in the news. You do not know why she is approaching you now.

A3. 17 *Bob*

Bob dropped out of college in his first year at the age of 18, 'with drug problems'. Around the time Bob was leaving he had seen a male colleague of yours for a few sessions. Bob is now 25, has returned to college and successfully completed the first year. He approaches the counselling service again but says nothing about having seen your colleague. You think you remember your colleague bringing 'Bob' to Group Supervision.

A3. 18 *Milly*

Milly has come to see you because she has just lost her job. She is close to tears. She tells you, miserably, that she saw a counsellor once at the Marriage Guidance Centre and it was 'most unhelpful ... useless, in fact'.

A3. 19 *Terry*

Terry has been referred to you by his GP for his anxiety. His previous counsellor, Julia, had to move rather suddenly to a town in the North. He reports in glowing tones the enormous help Julia had been to him ...

Beginnings: A session after a difficult previous session

Beginning a session after a difficult previous session clearly raises questions about the ending of the previous session! Tutors may therefore wish to use the examples in this section in conjunction with the difficult session ending, examples **A3.** *30–37.*

A3. 20 *Menoah*

You have been working with Menoah for about six weeks and she is gradually able to explore some of the painful memories of her childhood. As she approaches a particularly frightening memory, she becomes very agitated, jumps up and insists on leaving the counselling room and the building. You have the presence of mind to say 'See you next week' as she leaves, but it was not clear whether she heard you. It is now a few minutes before she is due for her next session ...

A3. 21 *Menoah*

(As 20 above.) ... You see Menoah arrive in the building looking very dishevelled five minutes before the counselling session is due to start.

A3. 22 *Gavin*

You had a sudden opportunity to take a short break and have come back feeling refreshed. You are aware that Gavin, who's been seeing you for about six months now, was angry that you went at such relatively short notice, and immediately before your holiday he left the session, slamming the door behind him. You are due to see him in five minutes.

A3. 23 *Mandy*

Mandy is very shy, very sensitive and exceedingly beautiful. She has been exploring with you her feelings of isolation and seems to be gaining confidence. At the end of the last session she told you she thought she might be falling in love with you. You were not sure how to respond and were glad it was the end of the session. You are about to see her again.

A3. 24 *Mr M.*

Mr M. reminds you somewhat of your father. Mr M. had been referred from his work setting and although he said that he was very glad to be seeing you for counselling you become increasingly unsure, during the first session, whom it is he's trying to please. Just as you are finishing the first session he says he finds you very attractive and is keen to return for another session. That second session is about to begin. . .

A3. 25 *Alistair* (see **A3.** 46)

Alistair came into counselling saying he thought he might not have grieved the death, twelve years previously, of his sister, Mona. He spent the first six months of counselling remembering, piecing together the memories of his fragmented childhood and making sense of the associated feelings. You remind him very gently that in a few weeks it will be the anniversary of her death. He becomes very angry at this point and threatens to leave counselling altogether. . .

Endings

Course members often struggle with the business of ending, whether ending a brief use of counselling skills, a contracted counselling session or a counselling relationship. Any ending involves parting and a loss of the intimacy which has been established. To recognise this loss and still to end confidently, firmly and with accepting warmth is an important and empowering part of the counselling approach. It can be a way of communicating a belief or trust in the client's capacity to contain and manage his own feelings and to grow from his own self-discovery. Endings can also touch off a whole range of feelings associated with loss, and course members may need to work on their own losses before they can become confident about working with the losses of others. For this reason they are likely to need considerable practice with managing endings.

Endings: First-session endings

A3. 26 *Mrs S.* (see **A3.** 1)
You have been listening for about forty minutes to Mrs S.'s fears and deep feelings of grief and despair about Seamus's handicap. You are aware that she is running out of steam and that you yourself, will have to be getting back to the other children. You want to finish off in a minute or two . . .

A3. 27 *Miranda* (see **A3.** 2)
Miranda has been expressing not just her sadness about her parents' separation but also her anger at her boyfriend's recent behaviour. She seems tired now and you, too, are tired after a long day. You want to bring the session to a close . . .

A3. 28 *Greg* (see **A3.** 5)
When you finally understand Greg's anger and, ultimately, his fear about the steroid treatment, you are able to talk him through the probable risk and side effects more realistically. He begins to appreciate that the medical risk was less then he had imagined and seems ready to leave your office . . .

A3. 29 *Arabella* (see **A3.** 8)
You have listened to Arabella's anger and helped her make some sense of her feelings. She now seems keen to come back and talk for a further six counselling sessions, starting the following Monday. You need to finish off the session quickly as you have come to the end of Arabella's time and have someone waiting.

Endings: More difficult sessions

A3. 30 *Josie-Ann*
You have listened to Josie-Ann and helped her make sense of her anger and her helpless feelings about not being promoted. She now seems keen to come back and see you again and you have arranged to see her for a number of counselling sessions starting next Wednesday. You need to finish off that session quickly as you have another appointment. Every time you try to finish she asks another question about counselling . . .

A3. 31 *Leon* (see **A3.** 6)
In talking with you, Leon has gained some awareness of his difficulties with trust and of the kinds of things which cut him to the quick and lead to his storming off. When you remind him that he has five minutes left you notice that he looks hurt for a split second and then seems to be on the point of storming off . . .

A3. 32 *Delia and Baldip*

Delia and Baldip are beginning to talk with each other with far greater honesty than ever before. You admire them for the risks they have taken to deal with some painful areas in their relationship. On this occasion, when you warn them that the end of the session is approaching, they both turn to you and say how much better they feel after their sessions with you. They tell you that they can't talk with each other half so easily without you, you are so warm and supportive and understand them both so well. They want to see you more often. Perhaps on Friday?

A3. 33 *Mr M.* (see **A3**. 24)

During the second session with Mr M. you enabled him to recognise his longing to be close to a woman and also to recognise his warm feelings towards you which he only knew how to express through sexual innuendoes. You are about to remind him that it is nearly time to end the session but before you can get in with your words he plunges into recounting deep fears about his wife leaving him. You can't get a word in edgeways.

A3. 34 *Sharon*

Sharon has been talking with you in this first session about her 'fascinating' job and all her responsibilities. She tells you a bit about her significant relationships and then, just as you are about to finish, she bursts into tears . . .

A3. 35 *Colin* (see **A3**. 3)

You have enabled Colin to express some of his feelings of fury towards the driver and also his sense of helplessness about the accident. You know that his leg will probably mend without further operations but there is a tiny chance that his knee will need further operations without, at this stage, a predictable outcome. He starts to ask lots of 'difficult' questions . . .

A3. 36 *Gina*

Gina has been making a lot of demands on your time in various different ways. You have negotiated three-quarters of an hour with her. Five minutes before the end, she tells you she has been made homeless and starts crying. You are expected elsewhere in ten minutes.

A3. 37 *Chris*

(Horseshoe Role Play)

Background for course members:
You've been seeing this person weekly for two months. It's nearing the end of the session.

'Chris'– played by the tutor:

> Nobody cares what happens to me. In between seeing you I feel so lonely. Do you realise there are 167 hours to wait until the next time. I just sit there sometimes and stare at the walls. It's not fair. Other people have friends and family to look after them. Why not me? Why can't you see me more often? If you really cared about me you would. But it's just a job to you, isn't it?

Ending counselling relationships

Counsellors may need help in expressing feelings of sadness at the ending while still clearly ending the relationship.

A3. 38 *Andrew*

Andrew has been having a lot of arguments with his parents recently. He approached you, the counsellor at college, as the rows were interfering with his college work. After six sessions he is much happier and has decided to move into a flat with his parents' support. He wishes this session to be his last.

A3. 39 *Grace*

Grace's mother died a year ago, having been ill with cancer for some time. Grace nursed her till she became too ill and was admitted to a hospice, where she died. Grace has been seeing you, a bereavement counsellor, for three months, is feeling a lot better and thinks counselling could stop soon.

A3. 40 *Menoah* (see **A3.** 20 and 21)

Menoah had been sexually abused as a child by her father. The memories of that early abuse had made it difficult for her to manage the intense associated feelings in the early stages of counselling. Menoah has now been working with you for nearly a year and is beginning to feel much more confident in herself and more in charge of her own feeling world. She wishes to finish counselling soon.

A3. 41 *Rehka* (see **A1.** 31)

After a difficult start, you and Rehka were able to explore her feelings, particularly her anger, in a way that made sense to her. This enabled her to feel generally more confident about herself and all her feelings. She has also been able to be more assertive with her family and to develop her own personal expectations of herself, rather than being so vulnerable to family expectations. She seems ready to leave counselling.

A3. 42 *Gary* (see **A1.** 17)

Gary has used counselling well to recognise that he was not guilty for the redundancy. Once he had understood and explored his initial fury, he also understood the naturalness of his underlying fear and recognised how much the redundancy had hurt his self-esteem. Knowing he was not guilty he has finally told his wife and discovers that it is indeed possible for them to face this challenge together. He no longer needs the counselling sessions.

More difficult counselling relationship endings

Counselling relationships which are difficult to end are often telling us something about unresolved grief in the client, and possibly also in the counsellor. Course members often need practice in thinking about such endings through case study discussion before moving on to practice responding in role plays.

A3. 43 *Grace*

Grace's mother died a year ago, having been ill with cancer for some time. Grace nursed her till she became too ill and was admitted to a hospice where she died. Grace has been seeing you for three months, is feeling a lot better and tells you her husband thinks it's time she stopped counselling.

Note: This is similar to **A3.** 39 above but, in this case, the husband's wishes, expressed as thoughts, may be getting in the way of Grace's, possibly mixed, feelings.

A3. 44 *Terry*

Terry lost his counsellor, Julia, soon after his partner had left him for another man. During counselling Terry had worked hard at exploring and understanding the many different and difficult feelings evoked by this complicated 'double loss' of both partner and first counsellor. He has, by and large, come to terms with these losses. However, when he realises that a longed-for promotion at work will take him away from you, his second counsellor, his anxiety starts to become incapacitating again. He has two months left in your town and has just missed a session.

A3. 45 *Naomi* (see **A1.** 29)

Naomi has eventually come to recognise her underlying feelings of hurt, rejection, loneliness and confusion, and also acknowledges her feeling world much more, understanding why she has needed to deny the feeling part of herself. One of the feelings Naomi still does not seem able to recognise or explore is envy. You will be giving up work in six weeks to have a baby and you have decided not to return to work for at least a year. You would like to be able to help Naomi face her feelings about your leaving and about your new baby . . .

A3. 46 *Alistair* (see **A3.** 25)

Alistair's sister died twelve years before he sought counselling and it was well into the second year of counselling before he could really let himself experience the feeling of grief relating to her loss. He plans to end counselling in six months but, as the end approaches, he finds himself again overwhelmed with extreme feelings of sadness and isolation.

A3. 47 *Brian*

You work as a volunteer with young people. Brian is 16 years old and has been 'chucked out' by his foster parents. Last night he slept rough and came into the centre today saying he wanted help in finding accommodation. He says he does not want a reconciliation with his foster parents. You think he ought to see someone else to get some more trained counselling help, but Brian says he trusts you, and doesn't want anything to do with 'social workers'.

A3. 48 *Gladstone and Rose*

You have worked with Gladstone and Rose for nearly six months. Gladstone came reluctantly, feeling pushed into counselling by Rose, but they seemed to work through this and Gladstone has expressed satisfaction at what they have achieved. He now wishes to finish counselling, but Rose wants them to continue.

Interruptions to the counselling relationship

Inevitably, on occasions, the counselling relationship will get interrupted and course members need to learn how to respond to the feelings inevitably evoked by these interruptions.

A3. 49 *Jill and Robert*

(Role Play)

Jill (client)

It's nearly five years now since your husband left but it took nearly three years to sort out the tangles of the divorce. At about that time your father became ill. He died just over eighteen months ago. On the anniversary of his death you began to feel that you couldn't go on coping. You struggled on your own for about three months till you finally decided to seek help from a counsellor – Robert.

You have been seeing Robert now for nearly three months and he's just about to go away on a short holiday so you'll miss your next two sessions. Your rational self recognises his right to holidays but deep down you're pretty furious with him for going away just at this stage. You're pretty reluctant to express your anger for fear that he might stop the sessions or that he might have you taken into hospital while he's away.

You're very frightened of the powerful feelings of depression and hopelessness which threaten to overwhelm you and you just can't bear to leave his office.

Robert (counsellor)

You are going away for a short holiday on Friday. (You're also feeling a little guilty about leaving your elderly mother behind.)

Jill referred herself about three months ago, saying she couldn't cope with the powerful feelings and the confusion surrounding the first anniversary of her father's death. A gradual recognition and acceptance of this loss seems to have awakened some of the powerful feelings she had not allowed herself to feel when she separated from her husband five years previously. She has been courageously exploring some of these feelings of despair and desertion. It is now forty minutes into your fifty-minute session ...

A3. 50 *Stella*

You have been seeing Stella for about six months and have just returned from a two-week holiday break. You thought she might have had feelings about your break but she had seemed pretty nonchalant about your holiday before you went off. Now that you are back she is almost unable to speak to you.

116

A3. 51 *Alison*

Alison has been rather difficult to engage in the counselling process but she is now, at last, coming regularly [and really working at exploring the feelings surrounding her sister's death two years previously in a car accident]. Her session is on a Monday and just at the moment you have no time on other days. For personal reasons you are suddenly obliged to cancel all next Monday's clients at short notice.

Note: The focus material in square brackets can give ideas about what might be awakened for Alison but can also be reserved to give the material more scope for imagination.

A3. 52 *Dean*

Dean's GP encouraged him to come and see you to talk about 'his depression'. Funding for the centre is extremely limited so most people pay for their counselling. Dean pays his bills absolutely regularly but keeps cancelling sessions ...

A4. ETHICS AND GOOD PRACTICE

The BAC Code of Ethics and Practice for Counsellors (1992) and *The Code of Ethics and Practice for Counselling Skills* (1989) aim to clarify those two different activities and the relevance of different ethical codes.

Although we have put 'Ethics' at the end of the Core Relationship Skills Section, ethical values are of course implicit, if not explicit in the resources of Section **A1–3**. Categorising resources which aim to look specifically at ethical issues is extremely difficult if not impossible, for while some case studies can be restricted to one fairly clear-cut issue, most raise a number of dilemmas which are often boundary issues. In fact, the most difficult resources to categorise are often those with the most learning potential.

Recognising this kind of overlap, we have put the resources into rough groupings which we hope will enable trainers to find, and then adapt, resources for their particular training needs. We hope that the resources here will stimulate discussion and open up new areas for consideration.

One way of working with ethical issues is to choose a selection of vignettes from the following subsections and ask the key questions:

a) *Which elements of the BAC Code apply?*

b) *How might you handle the situation?*

Referral

However brief the relationship with the referrer, referrals are always the 'end of the relationship' and thus constitute a loss. And however reasonable the reasons for referral, the person being referred almost always experiences feelings of rejection even if these are barely conscious. Useful key questions in the general context of 'Referrals' are likely to address:

- *ways of recognising and valuing the relationship's coming to an end;*
- *ways of reflecting possible feelings associated with loss;*
- *ways of reflecting possible feelings of rejection;*
- *demonstrating quiet confidence in the referral process.*

Referral from a role using counselling skills

A4. 1 *Mrs Wilson*

You are in the Ministry and have noticed that a choir member, Mrs Wilson, is sometimes unable to sing for tears. The family are all very involved with the church and you recently gathered from Mrs Wilson's daughter that some difficult secrets are beginning to emerge. Mrs Wilson seems to linger after choir practice one evening and you decide this might be the moment to raise the subject of getting help in a different context.

A4. 2 *Olivia*

Olivia is a highly articulate 27-year-old single mother who has had to interrupt her studies to give birth to her second child. She knows her way around the welfare system extremely well, yet has come to you at CAB ostensibly to ask your advice yet again about some detail of the housing benefit ruling. You believe that she is coping well with an extremely difficult situation but when you give her the information she has sought again she hurls verbal abuse at you and storms off. The next time she approaches you, you see that she has been crying and you decide to suggest the idea of getting some help.

A4. 3 *Callum and Catriona*

You come on to the ward one day and find Callum and Catriona with their backs to each other; she in tears and he with a stony expression. You discover their baby has just died.

Referral as a result of limitations in your own experience

A4. 4 *Duncan*

You have been working with Duncan for about three sessions and today you feel puzzled about his odd behaviour. He seems lifeless and listless. You feel increasingly uncomfortable about his capacity to relate to you and his difficulty with expressing feelings. You decide that you are too inexperienced to go on working with him and want to try to share this with him ...

A4. 5 *Heather*
(Horseshoe Role Play)

Tutor note: If you are a male tutor change Heather to Hector and adapt background notes accordingly.

Background given to course members:

You are a health visitor and have been seeing Heather regularly. You have built up a very good relationship using your counselling skills. You usually spend a little time with her, listening to her troubles, doubts and anxieties. On this occasion she tells you she has been having awful nightmares and has started remembering times in her childhood when her uncle had sex with her. You realise that you do not have enough training to help her with this yourself so you will need to make a referral.

Heather: Role played by tutor:

I don't know why I've suddenly started remembering these things. I wish I hadn't. But now I have, I can't stop thinking about it. And I'm having awful nightmares. They're getting so bad I don't want to go to sleep any more. What am I going to do?

Heather: Role continuation (if appropriate):

But I couldn't possibly tell anyone else. I've never been able to talk to anyone else like I am talking to you. I can't imagine saying any of this to a stranger! You're different. I can trust you. Someone else would probably think I'm going off my trolley. No . . . it wouldn't work.

A4. 6 *Pan*

Pan Nguyen is referred to you by his tutor because of his under-achievement in end-of-term exams. You attempt to work with him, but find it impossible to keep hold of what he is saying because you are struggling to understand him. He is becoming increasingly frustrated and you feel that your lack of comprehension and experience in understanding is adding to the difficulties for him.

Note: The tutor can here encourage exploration of the potential dilemma of whether it is wiser to risk the 'rejection' of referral or to face the 'difficulty in understanding' and work through that with Pan.

A4. 7 *Bogdan*

You have been working with a particular client for six weeks, and although you think you know what the 'problem' is, you don't feel you are making much progress. In fact you are beginning to feel awkward when this client arrives each week.

Note: Key questions might include: What role might supervision have in this case? How might you use this 'awkward' feeling in counselling?

Referral as a result of inappropriate professional and personal relationships

Note: The four vignettes below invite exploration of ethical practice and boundary issues.

A4. 8 *Craig*

Increasingly, a colleague has been confiding in you during break times but hasn't taken up your invitation to go somewhere quieter and talk. At the end of one break, he stands up to go and then says 'My partner walked out yesterday.' You are not sure what to do.

A4. 9 *Gareth*

Your job is divided between teaching English in a Sixth-Form College and work as the College Counsellor. Before you start teaching this year's intake of students a young man called Gareth approaches you in the counselling room in great distress. As he starts to tell his story you realise he is the Gareth Jones of your new English intake with whom you will be in close contact over the next two years.

A4. 10 *Mrs Yalom*

Mrs Yalom has come to you to try and understand why things are so difficult in her marriage and why it is that her grown-up children no longer come and visit them. In the course of the first session it emerges that Mr Yalom actually works at the same place as your partner and is a reasonably close colleague.

A4. 11 *Gwyneth*

You have been using your counselling skills in your interactions with Gwyneth and the relationship seems to be intensifying towards a contractual counselling relationship. One day she excitedly shows you her house plans and she tells you that they are about to move into a house in Rose Street. You live in Rose Street and realise with dismay that the house next door, which has just become vacant, is the one Gwyneth is about to move into.

Referral as a result of limitation of time or work overload

A4. 12 *Daz*

You work as a teacher and have just two hours each week on your timetable for counselling. One of the students, Daz, comes to you looking rather worried and asks to talk to you about the coming exams. You are already counselling three other students and, knowing that exam anxiety can be linked with other issues, you are worried about the time this may take.

A4. 13 *Mrs Jay*

You work as a Charge Nurse in a home for the elderly. The manager has given you a full day for your counselling work. You really appreciate the support she has given you for your counselling training and the encouragement she gives to your work. You are currently seeing five people on your 'counselling day', and Mrs Jay, who has heard how useful the counselling is from Mrs Adler, has approached you for counselling too. You know that the manager has been dropping hints to Mrs Jay for a while and you would like to please her, but you also know that five really is your maximum and you wouldn't be doing yourself – or them – justice by taking on a sixth person.

A4. 14 *Leslie and the Director*
(Role Plays)

Leslie

You work for a small counselling agency which helps people come to terms with loss. The agreed client load for each counsellor is a maximum of twenty clients per week. Because you are more experienced than your colleagues, you take the most 'difficult' clients and you are feeling quite stretched by your current caseload. There has recently been a disaster in a nearby town and your agency director is asking you to take on an extra five clients.

Agency director

You are the director of a counselling agency which helps people come to terms with loss. Your counsellors see a maximum of twenty clients per week and are working to full capacity. A few days ago there was a disaster in a nearby town and you have been asked by one of your funders to take on fifty crisis clients. Leslie is one of your best counsellors and you ask Leslie to take on five of these clients. This seems a reasonable request under these grievous circumstances and you are convinced that Leslie will accede to your request.

Referral as a result of limitations of a personal nature

Example key questions:

How would you feel in this situation?
What might you do?

Note: Sudden events can happen in a counsellor's own life at any point in a counselling relationship. Key questions might focus on whether supervision could enable the counsellor to continue working with Sasha.

A4. 15 *Sasha*

You have started back to work as a part-time counsellor in a General Practice. One of the patients, Sasha, has been working through the harrowing feelings of guilt and pain associated with the death three months earlier of her daughter Elizabeth. One day your own 15-month-old daughter falls down the stairs and gets concussed. The hospital wants to keep her under observation. Although she appears normal there is some lingering doubt about internal injuries. You are aware that your own worries and guilt feelings may make it impossible for you to give your full attention to Sasha.

Note: The following two cases involve temporary situations in the counsellor's life which are likely to resolve over time.

A4. 16 *Mr Read*

You work in a local Community Centre which has a long-standing Counselling Service. Six months ago your mother, aged 72, died of cancer and your father, who is 79, is not really managing but wants to struggle on his own. You really find it very distressing. Today Mr Read (80) comes into your centre wanting to see a counsellor, but once he starts to open up you realise he wants help with grieving the death of his 72-year-old wife and your own feelings begin to rise.

A4. 17 *Hamish*

You are a social worker attached to a busy Health Centre and Hamish, an 18-year-old college student came initially about three weeks ago to seek advice about housing. He's been back a couple of times and your use of counselling skills has enabled him to build up trust. He has mentioned 'depression' and you think he may be ready to accept a counselling contract. Meanwhile, however, your own 17-year-old son Hugh has dramatically left home, storming off at the beginning of his A-level year saying he is 'too depressed to live at home' and seeking housing elsewhere. You are really hurt and bewildered by this behaviour.

A4. 18 *Mrs Walker*

Mrs Walker has been approaching you at the centre where you work and you think she might be interested in agreeing to a more predictable counselling contract to explore her various difficulties. You bring up the subject and she seems keen to start. In the first session she starts to tell you about her secret drinking. Your mother, however, was also a secret drinker who eventually died a few years ago from a complicated alcohol-related disease and you know that the whole area is still very painful for you.

Referral to a more appropriate mode of working; to couples, to singles, to families, to long-term work

A4. 19 *Mr O.* (see **A3.** 15)

Mr O. has been having counselling sessions with you at the Church Counselling Service for about six months. He has been increasingly able to experience his own feelings about his daughter's miscarriage and his feelings about Mrs O.'s drinking. He is now understanding her more, and she, in her turn, is saying that she would like help in communicating better. You decide this is the moment to refer them to a colleague with training and experience in couple work.

A4. 20 *Mr Harris and Mrs Harris*

You work for a Counselling Service which takes individuals and couples. You have been seeing Bob and Beth Harris now for six sessions, which have gone very well, and they are opening up their feelings much more to one another. This growing closeness, however, has been a bit unnerving for Beth and has put her in touch with some difficult feelings about her own childhood. You think that these feelings might more usefully be explored in a one-to-one.

A4. 21 *Jaqui*

You are a social worker and your work sometimes brings you into contact with young people. Jaqui is a rather depressed 15-year-old who has been caught shoplifting for the second time, and the police have put her in touch with you. At first she seems reluctant to talk but she gradually begins to trust you and she tells you about who will do what with whom and who talks to whom and what she doesn't get in her family. You become concerned about the other children in the family and begin to wonder about family therapy.

Note: This referral study could be linked with family role plays in Section B.

A4. 22 *Richard*

Richard's GP has encouraged him to come along and talk to you about his feelings of depression. Richard tells you that one of the difficulties associated with being so depressed is that his partner, Paul, has been getting very irritable. Previously they both enjoyed going out and socialising – going to the theatre and so on – but now it is only Paul who is always dying to go out, have fun and be with their many friends, whereas Richard really only wants to be at home, preferably with Paul.

A4. 23 *Susanna*

You work part-time as a counsellor offering short-term counselling for the employees of your organisation. There is a strict limit on the number of sessions the employer will finance. Susanna has approached you for some sessions saying she thought her 'bulimia might be coming back'. Susanna is a highly sensitive, highly intelligent young woman who builds up a good relationship with you. As her story begins to unfold you realise that she has almost certainly been sexually abused.

A4. 24 *Katie and Moira*

You work at a drop-in centre where Katie and Moira have come to get help with their relationship. As they talk you become aware that Katie seems more troubled than Moira, and Moira is quite frightened by Katie's anorexic behaviour. Katie is still immensely involved with her mother who still rings her every night.

Note: It is important for the counsellor not to get prescriptive and controlling like Katie's mother, but to face Katie with certain choices.

Receiving referrals

This section has similarities with 'Beginnings: a session with someone referred from another person or agency' (**A3.** 11–15). Again, any feelings of loss and rejection will need to be worked with.

Example key questions:

Has this change really been necessary?

What are the reasons for the change?

What feelings will the referrer have to deal with?

How might you usefully work with the referrer to make a good transition?

What feelings might exist about the loss of the previous counsellor/counselling relationship?

Note: Section **A3.** 11–19 also offers resources for practising receiving referrals where the key questions would again focus on the feelings aroused in the client by the referral process.

A4. 25 *Gillian*

Gillian has recently moved to your area and received your name from the Student Counsellor in London whom she had approached about anxiety over her finals.

A4. 26 *Paramjit*

You are a trained counsellor. Your colleague, Paramjit, has attended a counselling skills course and often comes to you for support because you understand the way he works. On this occasion he is feeling 'out of his depth' with a particular client who has started to tell him about some very distressing childhood experiences.

A4. 27 *Alex*

Alex comes into your room and plonks down on the chair. S/he says s/he has been 'sent' by your colleague because s/he is being disruptive and will be kicked out of the Centre unless s/he sees you.

A4. 28 *Joan*

You receive a phone call from another counsellor who works in a detoxification unit. She is working well with this client but has to make a referral because the unit management has put a limit on the number of follow-up sessions their clients can have. She is very concerned about her client and finding it difficult to make the referral.

A4. 29 *Satnam*

(Horseshoe Role Play)

Background given to course members:
You are a trained counsellor working in a health service organisation. Satnam, who also works in your organisation, sees him/herself as a counsellor although s/he is not employed as a counsellor and has attended only a number of short counselling skills courses.

Satnam (played by tutor)

> I'm glad you've got time to see me. I had to talk to you about this patient. I think you should see him. I've tried some TA and some Gestalt with him and a bit of Rational Emotive stuff and he seems to be responding. He's a fascinating case. He was born in Egypt and his parents died when he was very young, so he came to live with his grandparents. Then they died, would you believe it, and he went to a children's home where they did the most unbelievable things to the kids ...

Boundaries

Within the fields of psychotherapy, counselling and using counselling skills each individual client or situation can present us with new issues or dilemmas to be considered. There is therefore an almost infinite number of boundary issues which could be discussed. Such themes are considered in much greater depth in Tim Bond, *Standards and Ethics for Counselling in Action* (Sage, London, 1993) and Windy Dryden and Brian Thorne (eds), *Training and Supervision for Counselling in Action* (Sage, London, 1991). In creating resources for thinking about such dilemmas and practising ways of managing them we have decided to focus the work as follows: first, on the creation and maintenance of the counselling relationship (in respect of various 'third parties'); second, on boundary breaks that can occur and need to be understood; and third, on boundary breaks which occur unethically and need to be considered.

Ultimately the aim of all forms of counselling is the empowerment of the client and nowhere is this more pertinent than in the ethical dimensions of boundaries. The predominant key question, then, throughout this section, will be concerned with what is, in the end, likely to be most empowering for the client. Other key questions are likely to address such dilemmas as role conflicts and relationships with other colleagues.

In using the materials for role play, tutors are likely to be focusing on the congruence and assertiveness skills necessary in the maintenance of boundaries.

Creating and maintaining the counselling relationship boundary with other professionals

A4. 30 *Linda*

You have been seeing Linda for about three weeks. She is currently very distressed and confused and is regularly tempted to take bits and pieces belonging to others. One of the cleaners at your workplace takes her rings off when she does dirty work and these have been stolen. The cleaner is convinced, because of the timing, that the thief is your client and has told your manager. Your manager calls you in and explains this, asking whether *you* think it could be your client.

A4. 31 *Fred and Francesca*

A colleague, Fred, who knows you are on a counselling course comes to ask you to see Francesca with whom he is having difficulty. He says that Francesca needs 'psycho-sexual' counselling because she keeps making inappropriate advances to others in the centre.

A4. 32 *Sandra and Trev*

(Role Play)

Counsellor

You are a college counsellor and have been seeing a student, Sandra (19), twice a week for two weeks as she works through her powerful feelings about her parents' divorce. She has particularly asked you not to contact Trev, her tutor whose concern she has found intrusive.

Suddenly one lunchtime Trev comes to your office and asks you whether Sandra has been to see you. He also asks whether Sandra's father has contacted you. He lets you know that her father has contacted him. He also tells you that Sandra has been missing classes. Whilst you respect the concern which Trev shows for his tutee you are aware that he does not appear to respect the confidentiality of the counselling relationship.

Trev

You are a lecturer and a personal tutor to a girl called Sandra (19) about whom you are enormously concerned and for whom you feel a bit frightened. Her father has been in contact with you. You think he is a sensible sort of chap and you think Sandra has been overdoing things a bit lately. You suspect Sandra may have gone to the counsellor and you do not approve. Sandra must be made to keep up with her classes!

A4. 33 *Betty*

A member of staff, Betty, makes an appointment to see you and complains about the behaviour of another colleague, Ben, who is a fairly close friend of yours. Betty has come to see you because Ben is a senior member of staff and she feels intimidated.

A4. 34 *Nigel and Nancy*

(Role Play)

Nigel

You are currently nursing a young man called Jamie who has found it very difficult to accept the diagnosis of his disease. He has just begun to take this news on board and has asked to see you. You have only now been able to find time to be with him and he has at last started to pour out his feelings. Suddenly there is a knock and Nurse Nancy comes in urgently wanting to discuss some 'worrying' blood results with you. She looks really worried [but you decide that it is more important to go on working with Jamie].

Note: The addition in brackets might be useful for a role play but could be left out for a case study in order to leave the discussion more open and allow for a key question such as: 'How might you handle Nigel's dilemma?'

Nancy

It has been very busy this week for you on this ward and you are ready for your leave this evening. Some blood results have just come through from pathology and there's one in particular, for Mrs S., that really concerns you and you'd like to discuss this with Nurse Nigel straight away. You can't find him at first, and then finally catch up with him talking to that difficult patient Jamie. You think Nigel has already given too much attention to Jamie and you consider Mrs S.'s results much more important.

A4. 35 *Dr F. and Frederika*

You work as a counsellor two days per week at a General Practice. Dr F. has recently joined the staff and is keen to use the counselling on offer in the practice for his patients. He has recently picked up that a young married woman called Frederika is deeply ambivalent about the prospect of having a baby. He has, it seems, made a good referral. However he approaches you in the reception and asks whether Frederika is becoming more organised yet about taking the pill.

A4. 36 *Private Practitioner Patsy*
(Horseshoe Role Play)

Background given to course members:
You are setting up in private practice and are pleased and flattered to get a phone call from a senior Social Services worker saying that you have been recommended as a counsellor. The worker is coming to see you about the client to be referred to you.

Senior Social Services Worker (played by tutor), who is brisk and businesslike.

> The woman I'm referring to you is called Xochelle. She has three young children and we've had to take them into care because she's been mistreating them. We want a report from you, of course, to say whether or not she's fit to have them back. How long do you think it will take?

A4. 37 *Director*
(Horseshoe Role Play)

Background given to course members:
You are the specialist counsellor employed by this organisation. Your main role is to work with clients of the organisation but you have also worked successfully with some of the employees and have established a good reputation. Today you receive a summons from the director.

Director (played by tutor) who is clearly rather uncomfortable and, consequently, a little brusque.

> Thank you for coming to see me. I can talk to you in confidence, can't I? It's about my deputy, James – James Doyle. I'm sure you've met him. I want you to see him for me. It's a slightly delicate situation, I'm afraid. He's rather gone off the rails since his wife died last year.

Further information about the role, to be used as appropriate: James and the director and their partners have been good friends, spending time together socially, so James's wife's death also affected the director. The director has been protecting James from the consequences of his poor work performance but is conscious that he cannot allow the work to continue going downhill.

Note to tutors: Trainee counsellors often have a variety of prejudices about 'managers', particularly that they are 'hard-hearted' and do not understand what clients need. In this role play, they often respond defensively to the request to 'see James' and may find it difficult to appreciate the extent to which, at that moment, the director is their client. The tutor may need to point out that the director is struggling with his own feelings and the tutor may want to replay the role so that course members have a successful experience of responding empathically and congruently to the 'Director' role.

Creating and maintaining the counselling relationship boundary with other people (relatives, friends, etc.)

A4. 38 *Valerie and Alan*

Valerie and Alan came to see you about the difficulties they have been having in their relationship. They were quickly able, in the first session, to recognise that Val found ambivalent feelings in the relationship particularly difficult. They wanted to separate for the moment, to give Val time to come to you separately for individual counselling. They plan to get together again in three months to 'try again' with their relationship. Valerie comes one day, announcing that she is pregnant and asking you to tell Alan as you 'still have his address'.

Note: This section can be used on its own as a case study for discussion, with the optional addition of the role play below. The tutor can also ask someone to observe the role play from the 'Alan' role, to bring in Alan's perceptions and feelings at the debriefing stage.

Valerie

You are a second-year student. You split from your boyfriend, Alan, four weeks ago and are still very hurt and feeling angry with him. You are also quite frightened of him. The counsellor, who is seeing you individually, seems very understanding. When you unexpectedly discover that you are pregnant, you are very frightened and can't bear the thought of telling Alan, so in your counselling session that afternoon you ask your counsellor to tell Alan on your behalf.

A4. 39 *Jane*

You have just spent an hour with Jane, who came because she has been asked to leave her job. Two years ago, while Jane was still at school, she admitted several thefts of small amounts of money. She still doesn't know why she did it (although her parents were going through a divorce at the time). She never spent the money and gave it all back.

Now thirty pounds has gone missing from the place where she works and the manager, who knows her history, suspects her. She was in great distress while telling you this and you are convinced that she's being truthful in saying that it wasn't her. She wants you to talk to her manager and save her job.

A4. 40 *Brian*

Brian is 16 years old and has been 'chucked out' by his foster parents. He has been in care most of his life. Last night he slept rough and he says he wants help in finding accommodation. He says he does not want a reconciliation with his foster parents. Neither does he want any contact with his social worker.

A4. 41 *Mehran and Jenny*

A 13-year-old girl, Mehran, asks to talk to you. She is very worried about her friend and doesn't know what to do. She felt she was being 'cold-shouldered' by her friend and they had a big argument which ended with her friend saying that her stepfather was 'interfering' with her and rushing off in tears. The friend's name is Jenny.

A4. 42 *Lazz*

Lazz says that by chance he saw someone take a ten-pound note from the pocket of someone else's coat. He was so stunned he pretended not to have seen it. He knows he should do something but is very worried about being involved in accusing someone of theft. He asks you to tell someone without giving his name.

Boundary breaks

In the following sections, situations are given where there may be a dilemma about the responsibilities of the counsellor to the client, to the organisation s/he works for, to other professional counsellors and to society as a whole.

Example instructions:

If you were the counsellor, how would you feel? What would be going through your head?

Which course of action would best meet:

> *The counsellor's needs or wishes?*
>
> *The client's needs or wishes?*
>
> *The organisation's needs or wishes?*
>
> *Society's needs or wishes?*

Read the vignettes below. In a group of three to five people, decide which elements of the BAC Code of Ethics and Practice for Counsellors apply. Which seems to your group to be the most ethical course of action to take?

Confidentiality

A4. 43 *Dick and Ch'ing-Fang*

You are working as a student counsellor with Dick who has been involved in a number of 'scrapes': 'borrowing' money from the Students' Union without proper authorisation, 'losing' an expensive college camera, claiming money from the DHSS in doubtful circumstances. You know his domestic situation is fairly desperate and that he is trying to support the woman he lives with, who is ill and has two small children.

One day an overseas student Ch'ing-Fang comes to your 'surgery' hour, very distressed and saying that three months earlier he went to the Students' Union for advice about a second-hand car. The person he saw offered to repair the car in return for £100 cash. The car has not been returned and he now wants to report it to the police but is frightened about doing so. You realise that he is talking about Dick.

Tutor note: It would be important to separate the tasks of empowering Ch'ing-Fang to use powers of the law to maintain his rights, and confronting Dick wherever possible with the material brought to the session.

A4. 44 *Florence*

You are a mentor at Florence's workplace. She tells you, in confidence, that a white member of your team is calling her names and making racist remarks (never in public). She is distressed and angry about this but begs you not to do anything in case the whole team 'turns against' her.

A4. 45 *John*

You are a social worker making regular visits to a single parent, John, who is depressed and frustrated on a low income and with no family or friends to turn to for help with the children. On this occasion he bursts into tears, telling you that he used his belt on his five-year-old and can't forgive himself. The child is covered with angry welts and bruises.

A4. 46 *Tim*

You work in a project for young people and you are Tim's key worker. Tim has a reputation for being a very 'difficult' young man and you are pleased that using your counselling skills has helped you to build up a good relationship with him. Central to the trust he has in you is that you have kept all his disclosures completely confidential. Today he is looking very pleased with himself and he tells you how he has ingeniously stolen a number of items from project workers. He sees from your face that you are shocked and he goes sullen and sulky, saying that if you tell anyone he'll never trust you or anyone else ever again.

A4. 47 *Leebert*

You have been working for a few weeks with Leebert, who is feeling very isolated and depressed after his girlfriend ditched him for Wesley. On this occasion he seems quite cheerful and asks you for your assurance that you will not tell anyone what he is about to say. You are so pleased he is feeling better that you agree without really thinking and he tells you to the last detail his plans to tamper with Wesley's car and cause a crash.

A4. 48 *Lucy*

Lucy has a degenerative disease which is causing her increasing pain and distress. One day you are delighted to find her calmer and happier. She wants to tell you something in complete confidence and you agree without really thinking. She then tells you in great detail how she plans to end her pain and distress through taking her own life.

Money issues

A4. 49 *Falah*

(Role Play)

Falah

You are desperately short of money. You are sure that you are entitled to Income Support but when you went to claim a couple of weeks ago you were made to feel like a criminal. You gave up after being ignored for over an hour and you can't face more public humiliation. You don't like asking to borrow money, but you are sure your counsellor will understand.

Counsellor

Falah has been coming to see you in the Agency for counselling young people. Today she comes in and asks if you can lend her some money.

A4. 50 *Mhairi*

Mhairi has come to you from the North. In the first session she tells you that she was paying her counsellor considerably more in the North than you charge your clients. You are particularly hard up at the moment and quite tempted to raise your fees to that of the counsellor in the North.

A4. 51 *Nick*

The centre you work for invoices the clients at the end of every month. Nick insists on writing out his cheque and paying at the beginning of the month. The administration are keen to accept his cheque.

A4. 52 *Ewan*

Ewan, who is now 26 and has a full-time job, has been referred to you for long-term counselling from a centre which is funded to work with young people up to the age of 25.

(a) He gasps when he hears your charges

4. 53 (b) He seems to accept your charges but his first cheque bounces.

4. 54 (c) He seems to accept your charges but on the due date for payment he has forgotten his cheque book and he has no cash. He promises to put it in the post but fails to do so.

4. 55 (d) He seems to accept your charges but on the due date for payment he has forgotten his cheque book and he has no cash. He promises to put it in the post and the cheque duly arrives. This has happened for three months now.

Presents

A4. 56 *Gabriel*

You work in an agency which offers free counselling. At the end of a session with Gabriel, who values considerably the work you have done together, he presses an envelope into your hand, saying 'I don't want you to feel obliged or embarrassed or anything. See you next week', and rushes away. The envelope contains £100 in cash.

A4. 57 *Philip*

Philip is a psychology student whose course tutor noticed that he seemed depressed and encouraged him to explore his depression through counselling. Philip arrives at each session with a different book which he wants to lend you. They are usually the most recent and most interesting books in counselling and psychotherapy.

A4. 58 *Primrose*

Primrose arrives on time, leaves on time, pays regularly and arrives at each session with a bunch of flowers for you.

A4. 59 *Sinclair*

Sinclair arrives at each session with a bunch of flowers, but always has some excuse for paying late for the session.

Sexual

A4. 60 *Alex*
You are seeing someone whose main concern is to do with intimacy. You gradually become aware of a growing warmth between you and of your own feelings of sexual attraction. At the end of what feels like a good session, Alex invites you home.

A4. 61 *Bernie*
Bernie has come to you to explore difficulties in getting close to people. You are committed to working with these difficulties even though you find Bernie physically rather repulsive. After a few weeks Bernie tells you of feelings of passionate sexual attraction towards you.

A4. 62 *Eve*
You have been working as a counsellor with a woman client for six weeks. She now discloses to you that she had a sexual relationship with her previous counsellor. He asked her a number of times whether she really wanted this and she said yes. She says she found him very attractive and feels responsible for the *affaire*. It was short-lived, however, because he became worried about his reputation. Now she feels hopeless because she has lost everything – again. Even her belief that she can be counselled. She says she always makes a mess of everything.

A4. 63 *Damien*
Damien is your colleague working in adult education. The people you work with are often lacking in confidence after being labelled 'failures' at school. You find Damien very patronising towards the women students, but some of them seem to enjoy his flirtatious approach. You are also inclined to be tolerant because he seems to give a lot of his own time to students after work. Yesterday, however, you saw him in the town holding hands with one of the students as they walked along together, laughing and talking.

SECTION B:
PRACTICE THEMES MATERIAL

B1–3 LOSS, BEREAVEMENT, CHANGE AND TRANSITION

(For other materials covering loss and bereavement, see also: **A1.** 17, 18, **A2.** 3, **A3.** 11, 12, 25, 33, 39, 43, 44, 45, 48, 51, **A4.** 3, 8, 14, 16.)

It is impossible to produce materials to illustrate all aspects of human loss. We have tried to cover a range of human losses from which trainers will be able to create more apposite materials where appropriate. This should enable groups to discuss the possible differences in meaning and effect of different losses on different individuals in different circumstances and at different times in the life-cycle. They can consider the effects of losses on partners and families and the effect of the different factors affecting loss.

These factors are further outlined in the Bereavement section. The first section here (**B1**) deals with a range of losses, section **B2** considers bereavement as a particular form of loss and section **B3** covers the various losses, as well as gains, associated with change and transition.

B1. LOSS (GENERAL)

Loss of 'objects' (purse, job, body-parts, home, culture, etc.)

B1. 1 *Mary Rose*

You have had your purse stolen recently, and although there was not much in it, there was a photograph of you and your close friend which is irreplaceable because she has since gone back to live in the Caribbean.

B1. 2 *Amy*

You were in a minor accident a couple of weeks ago. Although you were not hurt, you have lost your confidence in driving. You do not feel able to tell anyone because you had to overcome so much prejudice to learn to drive in the first place.

B1. 3 *Paul Smith*

(Role Play)

Counsellor

Mr Paul Smith is a middle-aged, well-dressed family man. You don't know why he has sought you out.

Paul

You are a man of about 40 and you have worked for your firm since you left school. Your line manager called you into her office last week to try to explain why it is necessary for the firm to make you and another colleague redundant in ten weeks' time.

One of your children is coming up to GCSEs, your wife's mother is quite ill and you haven't felt able to mention your redundancy at home yet.

You've come to a counsellor to seek help.

B1. 4 *Gordon*

You are a PE teacher and you have just had a leg amputated below the knee after a climbing accident in Glencoe. You don't yet know what is to become of you professionally. You are still grappling with this loss and with the sensation of a phantom limb. (You are not sure whether the careers counsellor could even begin to understand your plight.)

B1. 5 *Ruth and family*

Ruth

You have just come back from hospital having had a mastectomy. Your mother, Joan, has been looking after your husband and children while you've been away. You are now ready for her to go home but your mother is reluctant to do so.

You are frightened your husband will no longer find you attractive but find it difficult to talk to him about this issue.

Joan

Your daughter, Ruth, has been in hospital having a mastectomy and you've been staying at her house to look after your son-in-law, Tony, and your grandchildren.

You know that it is important after a major operation to take things slowly and you don't want Ruth to overstrain herself. You also sense tension between Ruth and Tony and are loath to leave them alone together.

Tony

Your wife, Ruth, has just returned from hospital having had a mastectomy. You are grateful to your mother-in-law, Joan, who has stayed with you to help look after the children but you are longing for her to return to her own place.

You are aware that Ruth is worried about her attractiveness but you don't know how to reassure her and you're not sure how you yourself will react to the change.

B1. 5 *Additional role*

Health visitor/district nurse

Your patient, Ruth, has just come home from hospital having had a mastectomy. As part of her aftercare, you have called round to see whether you can help in any way.

B1. 6 *The Corsini Family*
(Role Play)

Arturo (Father)
Your parents brought you and your sister to Britain as children from Italy where you still have uncles, aunts, cousins and even an aged grandmother. Although your family first settled in Scotland you have never really put down roots in one place and your job in the army enables you to keep moving on. You and your family have just been brought back from Germany to a posting in the South-West of England.

Gilly (Mother)
Your husband works in the army and although you liked it at first, you now find the unsettled life-style difficult to bear. You have just had a double tour in Germany, where you and the children were very happy, and have recently moved back to the South-West of England which sometimes seems even further than Germany from your family in Edinburgh. You are not sure how long you can stand this 'gypsy' life.

Jim (11)
Your dad's in the army and you have just returned from Germany where you had a really good time. Everyone's accent was different there so it didn't matter how you spoke but now you've moved back to a middle school in England where they laugh at your Scottish accent and the football isn't even any good. You are fed up.

Christine (16)
Your dad's in the army and you've just returned from six years in Germany where you had terrific friends and the life-style was excellent. You're utterly bored at your new school back in England.

B1. 7 *Stefan*
Stefan is an elderly man who came to England from Eastern Europe during the war and completely missed out on schooling. He has very pronounced ideas on education and frequently remarks to you that if only he had had the same chances as others, he would have risen to the top.

Loss of relationships

B1. 8 *Arnold*
You and your partner broke up six months ago. You know it's all over and it wasn't really working for a while before you broke up but sometimes it still hurts so much ...

B1. 9 *The Arnotts*

Penny and Ian Arnott had always got on pretty well together but had led increasingly separate emotional lives. When Ian met Avlette during his year in Brussels he and Penny decided to separate soon after his return and to file for divorce. He has recently been promoted and decided to buy a flat nearby where the children could visit him. Timmie (9) and Carla (7) are quite excited about their dad's new flat which has a swimming pool in the same block and is near a superb park. They find Avlette rather exotic. As Penny is telling you all this, it seems a very amicable arrangement ...

B1. 10 *Archie's mother*
(Role Play)

Archie's counsellor

Archie is a first-year student at the university where you are a college counsellor. He is having enormous difficulty settling into the university, which is over 100 miles from his home. His elderly father died just over a year ago. Archie is an only child and expresses guilt about leaving his mother alone at home. Although intellectually very capable he is thinking of giving up his studies and returning home. He has had difficulty finding accommodation but has recently found a place in a somewhat overcrowded house in a rather sleazy part of town. His mother rings you up to seek your advice about coming up to H. to help Archie and to sort out some suitable accommodation for him. You do not want to discuss Archie without his consent and you have an idea that the mother may be finding Archie's departure even more difficult than Archie.

Archie's mother

Your only son Archie has recently left home to go to the prestigious University of H. You are delighted that he got into H. and want him to do really well. Your husband died just over a year ago and you are managing pretty well on your own, but Archie's departure has left an awful hole in your life. When Archie rings up telling you of his awful accommodation problems and his thoughts about leaving university, you decide to go up and sort things out for him. He has mentioned a really understanding counsellor so you decide to ring the counsellor and ask for advice, hoping in secret that the counsellor may offer you some time when you are in H.

B1. 11 *Bill and family*
(Role Play)

May

Your son Bill has just been abandoned by his wife, Dawn, who has run away with Norman, an old family friend. You have gone to Bill's house to help with your grand-daughter Sarah, and are shocked at the state in which you find Sarah and Bill. You are outraged at Dawn's behaviour and very determined to reassure Bill. You keep trying to tell him that things will turn out all right in the end.

Bill

Your wife Dawn, has just left you and run away to London with Norman, one of your old family friends. You are still a bit stunned by the event, and are not sure how on earth you are going to manage with your daughter, Sarah, far less with your own feelings about Dawn and Norman. Your morally outraged mother (May) has come over to help but all she does is keep saying that everything 'will turn out all right in the end'.

Sarah

Your mum, Dawn, has left you and your dad, Bill. You haven't been getting on very well with mum recently and have occasionally wished you had a mum like your friend Shirley's. You are now certain the real reason mum left home is because you were making things so difficult. You try to be very solicitous to dad.

B1. 12 *Cyril and Lydia*
(Role Play)

Cyril

You love sailing and don't mind the cold, wet and danger. Your wife, Lydia, is less active than you, hates sailing and prefers doing nothing in the sun. She's recently been depressed and more than usually clingy, spending every minute of every weekend with you.

You've been asked to go on a sailing holiday at Easter with some good mates from the sailing club.

Lydia

You are feeling low after a long cold winter and you'd love to go off to the sun and be caressed by its warmth.

It's almost a year since your mother died and you're really experiencing the pain of that loss at the moment. You really don't want to be alone during the Spring holiday. Yet your husband, Cyril, loves sailing and really gets a kick out of the cold, wet and dangerous conditions. He's had a particularly stressful period at work and you suspect he'd rather go off sailing with his mates during the coming Spring holiday.

Note: These roles can also be used: in discussion, to consider the sense of loss in a marriage where people have differing needs; by creating two counsellor roles, to explore the counsellor's feelings when hearing one side of the story.

B1. 13 *Dave*

Dave's wife left him several weeks ago, taking their children with them. All his colleagues (including you) were very supportive at the time, knowing how shocked and upset he was. However, since then he seems to have lost interest in work. He misses deadlines, is offhand with people and rumours are circulating about his drinking. His colleagues are now fed up with his behaviour and two have approached you, as his line manager, to complain (unofficially).

Note: This vignette promotes discussion on the use of counselling skills in a management role and ethical practice in relation to role conflict and referral.

B2. BEREAVEMENT

There are many factors which will affect mourners after a death – age of the dead person, unexpectedness, place of death, type of death and so on. The single most important factor affecting the mourner is, of course, his or her relationship with the person who has died. We have attempted to structure this section to take account of the increasing complexity of the grieving process and have included at the end a few role plays of particular situations where grieving often goes unnoticed and can lead to symptoms of stress, anxiety and/or depression. We have left the most complicated losses with their concomitant stress, anxiety or depression to section **B7.** Within this section, Mrs T. in particular (**B2.** 16) demonstrates many factors which make grieving difficult.

Individuals and families

It is perhaps worth reminding course members that less experienced and particularly younger colleagues may have their first experience with death as part of their professional duties. Their capacity to make relationships with their patients or clients, and hence their grief when someone dies, is part of their humanity and therefore among their greatest professional assets.

B2. 1 *Student nurse*

A first-year student on your ward has spent a lot of time with a particular patient recently. This morning the patient died. You go into the linen room to find the nurse weeping. She says she knows it's silly but she can't stop crying and she doesn't want to appear like that on the ward.

Note: These two vignettes (**B2.** 2 and **B2.** 3) could be used to highlight differences in grieving patterns for men and women and the effect on grieving of more complex and ambivalent family relationships.

B2. 2 *Annabelle* (75)

Annabelle's husband Thierry (78) died of pneumonia in February. She is part of an easy, loving family and she is able to talk with them about Thierry, crying and sharing memories. She has come to see you about practical matters, finding it difficult to take on the administrative role which Thierry always played.

B2. 3 *Gerhard* (64)

Gerhard's mother, Mrs Z., is a sprightly 83-year-old who never really approved of her elder son's marriage to Ulrike, forty years ago. Ulrike died last month from secondaries of a cancer which she had had for some years. The end, however, came very quickly. Gerhard is complaining of back pains.

Note: The first of the following vignettes can be used to highlight fairly 'ordinary' grieving patterns as for instance when an elderly grandparent dies. Later examples are of more complex family situations where the adults may be so overwhelmed with grief or caught up in denial as to be virtually unavailable for the grieving children.

B2. 4 *The Kays*

Mrs Kay was 88 and had suffered from severe arthritis for several years. She had begun to dement slightly and then, when all the family were gathered for her 89th birthday, she suffered a stroke and died a few hours later. She left two sons, Keith and Konrad and their wives and families with each of whom she had enjoyed loving and individual relationships. On the anniversary of Mrs Kay's death, the family met at the graveside and a number of them cried. They then went to the pub and everyone thoroughly enjoyed the reunion. Telling you about this, Keith seems unsure whether it was 'right' to do it.

B2. 5 *The Green family*
(Role Play)

Barbara

You are 14. Your dad has just died after a year's struggle with cancer. You find yourself continually wanting to go out with your friends and get away from home to 'do your own thing'. Sometimes you feel bad that you might be hurting your mother. You are annoyed with your older sister because she refuses to discuss things about your dad's death.

Rachel

You are 16 and are in the sixth form. Your father died of cancer just before the school year started. You were, in a sense, his favourite and you feel the loss deeply. You find it hard to express your feelings. When your family wants to talk about your dad's death, you withdraw.

Callum

You are 18 and your father has just died after a year-long struggle with cancer. It is only a few weeks before you are to enter college and you are feeling anxious about leaving home for the first time, as well as anxious about going to college. You have experienced panic several times. You are not sure you should be leaving home and going to college rather than getting a job to help your family financially. You think it is not adult for a man to cry.

Mother

You are left with three children, Callum aged 18, who is just entering college, Rachel, 16 and another daughter, Barbara, 14. You are concerned about how you are going to make it financially and how you are going to cope emotionally without your husband. You are also in touch with some anger at your husband dying and leaving you with all of this responsibility. This feeling scares you. You are concerned about your son's leaving home, your older daughter's inability to express her grief and your younger daughter's apparent alienation from the family.

Listener (optional role)

You have been asked by Mrs Green, who has recently lost her husband after a year's illness with cancer, to sit down with her and her three children – a son aged 18, a daughter 16, and another daughter 14 – and help them to discuss their feelings and make realistic plans for the future. Mrs Green feels overwhelmed by the situation. Your task is to help them to express their grief.

B2. 6 *The Smiths* (Role Play)

Jean (mother)

You are 40 and over recent months your very sporty son, Angus (19), has been complaining of tiredness and pain in his legs. Last week at the hospital, after a long series of tests, he was diagnosed as having an incurable form of bone cancer. You've read something recently about scientific developments with genes or something which relates to cancer and you think that perhaps they'll have a cure in time to save Angus and you've told him this. Your husband, Bob, seems to be awfully busy at work and your other son, Jamie (17), is being increasingly rude and disobedient again, just when he seemed to be getting over it.

Bob (father)

You are 44 and your son Angus (19) has just been diagnosed as having bone cancer. You know from reading and what you've been told that this particular cancer is incurable and that he has between three and six months to live. Angus is your firstborn son, you cannot face the thought of his dying so you pile on the work and try to forget. Your wife, Jean, and the boys keep talking about 'cures' and you think you ought not to challenge them so the 'extra work' keeps them at bay too.

Angus

You are 19, you play football for your local team and have represented your county at long-distance running. Last year your performance started to deteriorate and your increasing tiredness over recent months has meant you've had to have hospital tests. Last week they said you had 'bone cancer' which was a bit of a shock as you thought cancer was a killer, but your mum says they have just discovered a cure and you hope they'll get the new medicine to your hospital in time. You're not sure whether your dad's reluctance to answer your questions about the cancer is because he's so busy or because he's cross with you for something.

Jamie

You are 17 and Angus (19) your older brother is a brilliant footballer and cross-country runner. You've always looked up to him and sometimes even hated him for being so much better at everything. Now they say he's got cancer. You thought people died of cancer but your mum thinks that they can cure it and he won't die. Your thoughts are all muddled about this and you wish you could talk to your dad but he seems to be avoiding you and you've started to wonder if you've done something wrong.

Anna Grant (optional role)

You are 18 and your boyfriend Angus (19) was told last week that he had incurable bone cancer. You had secretly been hoping to get engaged at New Year and now your world seems to have fallen apart. Your mum, who wasn't that keen on Angus anyway, says 'There are other fish in the sea' and your dad, who knows Angus's father, Bob, just keeps saying 'I'll have to go and have a drink with Bob.' You then remember that your own natural father (John Smith) was also 19 when he died and you're not sure how he died and you keep thinking about him. Your step-dad has been just like a 'dad' for you and you're seen as 'just one of the Grants'. Your mind's a whirl but you feel you can't burden Angus with this as he has enough already – you don't know where to turn.

B2. 7 *Timothy's family*
(Role Play)

Alison (mother)

Your only son, 8-year-old Timothy, was killed in a road traffic accident three months ago. Since then you have been depressed and you often cry. You have lost interest in most of your friends and spend your time alone. You are angry with your husband because since Timothy's death he has kept himself busy and is unavailable to you. You are also angry because he wants another child right away. You feel this is insensitive and your relationship is becoming strained.

George (father)

Your only son, 8-year-old Timothy, was killed in a road traffic accident three months ago. You handle your grief by keeping busy both at work and in leisure-time pursuits. This annoys your wife, but you feel that keeping busy is all that is keeping you together. You would like to have another child soon but your wife is not interested in any more children who might put her through a loss like the one you've both just experienced.

Judy

You are 15 and your 8-year-old brother, Timothy, was killed in a road traffic accident three months ago. You miss Timothy, but you feel you mustn't talk about him to mum and dad. You're cross with them because all they do is argue about whether to have another child. (*Optional addition of neighbour role:* You've been talking to your neighbour, who understands people's feelings, and have asked her to come and talk to your parents.)

Neighbour

Ali and George moved in next door eight years ago, just before Timothy was born. Three months ago Timothy was killed in a road traffic accident. You've been a bit frightened of talking to them as you feel there is nothing you can do to help, although you have been showing your sympathy by doing little things for them. Their other child, Judy (15), has asked you to go and have a word with her parents as she is worried about them. You are currently on a counselling skills course.

B2. 8 *Jez*

You are 32 and your partner died suddenly just over a year ago, leaving you with two children, a girl aged 6 and a boy aged 4. A colleague at work seems to be angling for a closer friendship. You have come to a counsellor because you don't seem to know what to do, encourage the advances or rebuff them. In any event you can't get the thoughts out of your mind.

Note: Even where bereavement is recognised and is not repressed from memory it takes time for the process of mourning to take its course. Some people may be unable to experience the loneliness of bereavement and may rush into new relationships before they are ready, others may never get through the grief and may never risk another relationship. Jez's situation can be used to reflect on readiness for this difficult transition back into relationships. Jez can be either male or female. There may well be differences in response and in readiness between men and women.

Bereavements which easily go 'unnoticed' or unrecognised: gay and lesbian bereavement

The advent of AIDS has helped raise general awareness of gay bereavements. None the less there are non-AIDS-related deaths which may be ignored. Key questions should address the feelings of the person bereaved and any difficulties experienced by course members in entering their frame of reference.

B2. 9 *Sue and Ginny*

Sue had lived with Ginny for over nine years and when one night Ginny did not return from a coach trip to the theatre in London, Sue became very anxious. She eventually rang the police and discovered there had been a bad accident on the motorway involving a coach. It was a filthy night and by the time Sue got to the scene of the accident all the severely injured had been taken to hospital. When Sue got to the hospital she discovered that Ginny had already died. The police had rung Ginny's brother, who had never really accepted her relationship with Sue. Hospital staff turned to her brother to make the arrangements surrounding Ginny's death and he just went ahead without consulting Sue. Sue has come to you complaining of headaches.

B2. 10 *Ben*
(Role Play)

You and Tanu were lovers. Tanu was married to a woman who, like him, was very young when they had their children. Nine years ago she left Tanu and the two babies when she discovered that Tanu was having a homosexual relationship with you. She has not made contact since but you believe that she went to live and work abroad. Shortly afterwards, you moved in. Your heart went out to the children and you were very supportive to Tanu in helping the older one to get over her difficult behaviour at losing her mother, and in caring for the baby. You, Tanu and the children became a loving family, with the children relating to you as a parent. Now Tanu has died, everyone seems to be assuming that the children will go to his mother or his sister. But they are *your* children ...

B2. 11 *Carla*
(Role Play)

You fell in love with Zofia over thirty years ago and lived with her for more than twenty-five. The idea that you might be lesbians did not seem to enter the heads of your neighbours, who seemed to see you simply as two 'spinster ladies' sharing a house for convenience. With Zofia's death last year, your world seemed to fall apart and you are achingly lonely. Everyone was very kind at the time but they expect you to be over it by now and seem irritated when you are not cheerful.

B2. 12 *Simon and Jeremy*
Simon's prestigious job took him overseas a lot and while he was away Jeremy would sometimes fabricate some slightly 'quaint' but also potentially dangerous sexual practices. Once, after Simon had been on a tour in Russia and was able to phone only sporadically, he returned home to find his flat full of policemen and to be told that Jeremy's body had been taken for a post mortem.

Bereavements which easily go 'unnoticed' or unrecognised: miscarriage, abortion, stillbirth

Nowadays there is greater recognition of the importance of grieving the life, whatever the import and meaning of that life, which has been lost. We have therefore chosen examples illustrating such bereavement, which may have happened at a time or in circumstances where the loss was not recognised.

B2. 13 *Sigrid* (37)

Sigrid at 17 had just started going out with Pierre. When her period was ten days late her parents panicked and rushed them into an immediate marriage. Three weeks later Sigrid did not want to marry Pierre but had felt guilty at having had a sexual relationship before marriage and at having tried to bring on her period by the old methods of falling off tables and having very hot baths. Three days before the marriage date her 'period' arrived, but she was so overwrought by this time that she had neither the strength nor the courage to refuse the marriage. It was never clear whether she had in fact been pregnant, but she then went on to have three (further) miscarriages before deciding to give up on the idea of having children at all. She had thought that the miscarriages were perhaps a 'punishment' for her early sexuality or for her attempts to 'bring on' her period, so she quickly put them out of her mind and got on with her studies. Now 37 and still in her rather miserable marriage with Pierre, she has sunk into a deep depression after the death of her 13-year-old dog, Micky.

B2. 14 *Nicola*

Nicola studied German and towards the end of her year in Munich realised she was pregnant by her violinist boyfriend Detlev. She was romantically in love with Detlev but realised that she did not want to marry him or stay in Germany and decided to come back to Britain, have an abortion and go into her final year. Soon after finishing her degree she married Arthur and had three healthy children. She has never really talked to Arthur about her time in Germany. David, the eldest, really 'took off' with the violin at about 13 and she began to get depressed.

B2. 15 *Agatha*

Agatha and Simon had a stillborn child while they lived in Ireland and life was hard. They then moved to England, worked hard, had their children who all did well, and they felt that life had been good to them. Now that their children are grown up they have gone back to where they used to live in Ireland. Now Agatha has started to cry and does not seem able to stop.

Bereavements which easily go 'unnoticed' or unrecognised: multiple ungrieved losses

Note: Mrs T. presents a particularly challenging situation. The previously ungrieved loss of the stillbirth in her youth will render other losses difficult to grieve, while also meaning that there are no children to help her and be with her in her grief over her husband, her own fear of cancer and the other frightening situations she is facing, which lead to even further denial. It is perhaps not surprising that all of this is being expressed through various symptoms.

B2. 16 *Mrs T.*

Mrs T. is still dressed in her night-clothes when you call to see her at 1.30 pm. Although she is only in her mid-50s she looks about 70. She spends a lot of time looking down at the floor, twisting her fingers or running them through her hair.

She and her husband had both been teachers and took early retirement a year ago. They had an active social life and tended to go everywhere together. She was unable to have children after one stillbirth, which she now finds herself thinking about constantly, although at the time it happened everyone congratulated her on coping so well.

Three years ago she developed breast cancer and, as a result, had three operations. Her husband was extremely loving and supportive during her illness but she became agoraphobic for a while.

Just as she was beginning to feel that she was getting better, her husband developed angina. He had an unexpected and fatal heart attack a week before the previous Christmas. Mrs T. spent Christmas alone, although her sister-in-law had invited her to stay with her. She has just spent two weeks in a psychiatric unit because she felt unable to cope. She has been discharged and is on a course of anti-depressants. She mentions attempts at suicide soon after her husband's death in her desire to be reunited with him. She tells you she had been unable to say very much about this to the doctor because she didn't feel he had time to listen.

While she was in the psychiatric unit, one of her neighbours arranged for a builder to replace her window frames. On returning home she found that a lot of her husband's property had disappeared from the garage. She has not told the police as she does not want to involve the neighbour, with whom she is friendly. She is also worried about the tree overhanging her garden from her neighbour's side. She says her friends and neighbours call and try to be helpful but they act as if her husband never existed.

B3. CHANGE AND TRANSITION

Adolescence and leaving home

The loss associated with many kinds of change and transition is often not recognised. This unrecognised loss can make change unnecessarily complex. Rituals which previously helped us through the period of extreme change and transition which constitutes adolescence have now largely died out. We have given examples here of some of the changes associated with adolescents and their families.

B3. 1 *Jenny*

You are 16 and have done rather better in your GCSEs than either you or your school expected, including an 'A' grade pass in Art. You've always rather wanted to do Art, but you were never sure you had any talent. You feel that your identity is very tied up with being an artist.

Your parents think that Art is 'all very well, but it won't get you a decent job' and they are discouraging you strongly. They want you to do 'academic' A-levels and go on to university. School seems to be keen on that plan as well.

You don't know what to do and ask to talk to the school counsellor.

B3. 2 *Ayinka, Des, Betty*
(Role Play)

Ayinka

You have just left home and boyfriend to go away to college. You are enjoying college life so much that it is hard to fit in your social life around your work. Your mother and boyfriend are ringing regularly and keep asking you to go home for the weekend. You find you don't want to go.

Des

Your girlfriend has left your home town to go away to college. You thought she might not stick it out, but she seems to be having such a good time she doesn't want to come home. You ring regularly.

Betty

Your daughter has just left for college and although you wanted her to go (or at least you thought you did), you find yourself worrying about her all the time and, particularly, you worry about the relationship with her boyfriend. You ring regularly but she doesn't seem to want to come home.

B3. 3 *Faisal*
You are 17 years old. Your parents are continually bickering and rowing and both try to get you on their 'side'. You've been hoping for some time that it will sort itself out but it is making you so confused and unhappy that you just can't stand it any longer. You want to know whether, legally, you can leave home.

B3. 4 *Yvonne*
You are a 16-year-old girl and have been going steady with Brian for the last twelve months. Three months ago at a party you had a row with Brian and ended up going to bed with another lad.

You can't tell Brian you've had sexual intercourse with someone else as he's told you he'd pack you in if you had sex with anyone else but him.

Now you realise you are pregnant and are not sure who the father is.

Finally, at your wits end, you arrange to see the counsellor and all you can do is sit in the chair and sob and sob.

B3. 5 *Ali*
Ali is 16 years old and has been 'chucked out' by his foster parents. He has been in care most of his life. Last night he slept rough and he says he wants help in finding accommodation. He says he does not want a reconciliation with his foster parents.

Additions to the family

B3. 6 *Romnauld and Julia*
Romnauld and Julia have been married for three years. They travelled a lot and led interesting and varied lives. They were delighted when Julia became pregnant but as the day approached when another human being was about to join their family, they found themselves wondering whether they'd done the right thing. Julia now wants to turn the clock back. Romnauld is absorbed in the baby from the minute he gets back from work but she dislikes the whole business of nappies and feeds and being tied down. You find her in tears . . .

B3. 7 *Patrick and Sylvie*
Patrick's wife Helene had left him to rush off to a romantic wandering life. Patrick continued to rebuild his old farmhouse home to make a life for himself and his children. About two years later he met Sylvie who agreed after a year or so to come to live with and look after the children. People said to the children, 'Aren't you lucky to have a new mum!' . . . but, six months later, Nadine, the eldest, is sulky and withdrawn.

B3. 8 *Batouk*

Batouk's second daughter has just left home to go to college in another town. They have been very close, particularly since Batouk's husband died suddenly last year. Batouk's ageing mother, Mrs P., can no longer manage on her own and although she wants to be 'independent' she is beginning to dement and Batouk knows she must take her in to live with her...

B3. 9 *Bobby*

Your son, Bobby went off to university nearly four years ago and graduated last summer. Since then he has tried very hard to get a job in his field and has been prepared to go anywhere in the country. However he has not been successful and has now returned home to the dole and not much prospect of work. He is beginning to stay in bed till midday...

B3. 10 *Leila*

Your husband has been in prison for nine months and is due to come home on parole next month. Your next visit is due tomorrow. You are feeling very mixed about his coming home and this is making you panicky about tomorrow's visit. You wonder whether you really have to go tomorrow and have come to discuss things with the probation officer who was sympathetic in the past.

Changing patterns of health, ageing and employment

B3. 11 *Mr Jones* (62)

'It's not bad when it's cold but as soon as the hot weather comes on I get all breathless. It takes me half an hour to get here from our house and you know how near that is. I seem to get pins and needles in my arm as well. I've got to go to the doctor on Friday. Do you know what he said to me last week. "I think you're a marvellous man, Mr Jones, to keep so cheerful." You see I never complain, but it can be a bit trying sometimes. By the time I got in last week I'd got palpitations – they were that bad I felt as though I'd have to call him out ...'

B3. 12 *Mrs Davis*

Mrs Davis has led a very active life as a postie, as a wife and mother and as a gardener and housewife. Now that her arthritis is getting worse she is no longer able to do her postie job by bike and has to do sorting work in the office. She hasn't the energy to give to the garden and even her grandchildren wear her out sometimes. She is aware that she is getting older, but everyone keeps saying how wonderful she is. She tells you she is fine, but you see how tired and washed-out she looks.

B3. 13 *Liz*

Liz is in her late twenties and has attended your group every week for the past six months. She has progressed rapidly in that time and has become noticeably more self-confident and outgoing. She is now thinking of leaving the group but is not clear in her own mind why. Her husband doesn't like her going out alone (although they rarely go out together). He doesn't go out drinking, she says, and always gives her his wage packet unopened. She feels that the house and their two pre-school-age children are her responsibility and worries about them waking when she isn't there.

B3. 14 *Naomi*

'You know I really have got a lot out of working in the evenings even though I get paid a pittance. I feel as though I'm getting my confidence back at last. But I feel really bad about leaving Dave with the kids. *They* don't want me to go out – *he* looks fed up with the whole thing. He's a good husband but he just doesn't have much idea about looking after kids. I feel as though I'm letting them all down. None of his mates seems to stay in while their wives go out and I think he's starting to resent it.'

B4. SEXUALITY

(*For other materials covering sexuality, see also:* **A1.** 23, **A2.** 13, **A3.** 23, 24, 33, **B2.** 8.)

It is important for those learning about counselling to be able to talk about sexuality and in particular their own sexual feelings. Unless people are able to talk about their own sexual feelings to a relative stranger they will be unable truly to listen to the feelings and fears of others. We would therefore encourage an approach which starts off with case materials, allowing a thorough exploration of attitudes towards a number of aspects of sexuality, and then moves on to role play to enable course members to identify with, and talk about, sexual feelings at different ages and in different contexts. Listening without judging is an important aspect of helping people come to terms with their own feelings about their sexuality.

The studies in the first section here focus more on adolescent sexuality and on coming to terms with sexual identity. In the second section the studies consider the role of sexual feelings and behaviour within long-term relationships in old age.

Sexual difference and sometimes sexual attractiveness can be exploited and power abused. The studies in the third section allow consideration of such issues and recognition of the feelings concerned.

Discovering sexuality

B4. 1 *Morag*

Morag is 17. She had too much to drink at a party six months ago and had sex with a lad she hadn't met before. She feels very ashamed of herself for enjoying it, because her mother has always told her it is cheap to have sex before marriage. (Her parents both get very embarrassed when they try to talk about sex.)

She has slept with two other young men since then and enjoyed that too, but she has just found out that people think she's a 'slag'.

B4. 2 *Cheryl*

'Before you start, I'm a lesbian. I don't want to change. I'm perfectly happy as I am. So if you don't like it, I'll go.'

B4. 3 *Gary*

Gary is 19. His friends seem to spend most of their time trying to find girls to sleep with. Although he has had sex with a few girls, he didn't find it particularly exciting. He's worried that there's something wrong with him.

B4. 4 *Paramjit*

(Role Play)

You are going to be married in the near future to an attractive man chosen by your parents. You are very happy in general but as the day comes closer, your nagging doubts about the sex act are getting stronger. You know the bare facts but have never heard your adult relatives talk about sex. You have picked up from your mother and aunt that it is a painful duty which must be borne without complaint. You want to talk about it to the counsellor and, at the same time, you are extremely embarrassed.

B4. 5 *Joshua*

'I decided I was going to tell you today, man... I just don't know... Every time I come I go away and I've still not... It's like... Oh shit. I think I'm queer. You know...? Like I get turned on by guys. I'm a... big... black... poofter. I've tried to like women – well I *do* like women but not... *that's* why I can't go out any more. How can I?'

B4. 6 *Mary Ann*
(Role Play)

You are 19 and unlike any of your friends you have had no sexual experience. You have recently met Paul (21) who is also pretty inexperienced. You have some physical sensations when you become sexually excited which are on the verge of being painful and you are wondering whether you could talk to someone at your GP practice.

GP/Practice nurse (middle-aged)
Mary Ann (19) has made an appointment but you think you may have picked up a look of disappointment when she saw you. You're not really sure what she's here for.

Sex and relationships

In general as a sense of sexual identity develops, more committed sexual relationships become established. Some difficulties in talking about sexual feelings and sexual longings in a relationship may have more to do with communication difficulties in the relationship than with actual sexuality itself. If clients are able to begin to talk more openly about their sexual feelings within the non-judgemental atmosphere of the counselling relationship, they may then be able to talk more openly to their partners. If not, then a referral to a marital–sexual therapist may be more appropriate – see Referral p. 119.

B4. 7 *Jean*

Jean is making her second visit to the clinic to talk about PMT. (The first time she had to rush off because her children were waiting outside in the car.) She is a single mother, and the way she shouts at her children when she feels pre-menstrual makes her feel awful. She describes her symptoms and the various treatments she has tried. Jean says that she has a boyfriend and is trying to decide whether to sleep with him or not. She is concerned that, though he is not pressurising her at all, once he got 'what he wanted' he might drop her. On the other hand, she wants to have a sexual relationship and isn't particularly interested in keeping him as a permanent fixture in her life. She is worried about her weight, and fears that if he sees how thin she is without her clothes he would be put off.

B4. 8 *Surinder*

Surinder comes to the clinic asking to see the woman doctor. She looks very doubtful about whether to stay after being told that there is no doctor at the clinic this evening. She explains that she has come to ask for something to help with her menopause symptoms. When prompted, she describes her symptoms which are to do with feeling tired and irritable at home. Surinder leads a busy life. She enjoys her job and has one or two good friends at work. The problem, it eventually emerges, is with her relationship with her husband. Her husband does nothing in the house, they hardly ever go out together and have nothing to say to each other. Despite this he is very demanding sexually and this is what is really getting Surinder down. She has not enjoyed sex for many years. Lately she has been staying up late in the hope that he will be asleep when she gets to bed but the more she tries to avoid him, the more aware of it and demanding he seems to be. Surinder is exhausted.

B4. 9 *Mary*

'We've been together twelve years and it's a really good relationship but he seems to have gone off sex. I've tried to be patient and loving like the books say, but it's really frustrating. Sometimes we start but he goes off in the middle and that's even worse. He feels guilty about it and I don't want to hurt him but I've been wondering whether I should have an affair. I'd rather make love with him, but I'm going bananas thinking he may never get it up again.'

B4. 10 *Gareth/Holly*
(Horseshoe Role Play)

Gay/lesbian client (played by tutor)

'My parents are coming to stay next week and I'm a bit worried. They've never met (Gareth *if tutor is male*, Holly *if tutor is female*) before. We've only got the two bedrooms. Gareth/Holly is looking forward to meeting them. I hope it goes okay.'

Note: The purpose of this role play is to look at what stops course members from 'naming' their speculation. The tutor 'client' deliberately skirts around the issue and may explain that the client will be reluctant to open up to someone who does not show acceptance by 'hearing' what s/he is saying, however obliquely s/he is saying it.

Sexuality and abuse of power

Sexual abuse of any kind has more to do with aggression and abuse of power than with sexuality itself, but we have put this material in this section because the two issues are so often confused and because abuse relating to sexuality can have effects upon the feelings of the abused person about their own sexuality.

B4. 11 *Wendy*

Note: It may be useful in working with Wendy to focus on her possible feelings of invasion and helplessness. As these become recognised, her feelings of anger are likely to grow and discussion can then emerge about how to manage the feelings of anger and use them most constructively in a delicate situation which may indeed have elements of powerlessness in it. In this vignette, Wendy's confidence in the validity of her own feelings will be paramount.

Wendy asks to talk to her office skills tutor because she is worried about the way her male supervisor at work 'flirts' with her. She wants to leave but is concerned that she will not easily get another job.

B4. 12 *Joan*
(Role Play)

You were raped as a child on a number of occasions by your uncle. In your early twenties, you realised that you were avoiding relationships which might lead to sex, and saw a counsellor for over a year. You have been in a loving sexual relationship now for eighteen months and have just discovered that you are pregnant. Suddenly you are filled with fear for the child and you find yourself looking at all adult men with suspicion and making plans to keep them out of your house. When you catch yourself wondering about your partner, you decide to go again for counselling.

B4. 13 *Mayo*
(Role Play)

You are 23, married with one child and another on the way. You love your job and are keen to get promoted and established in the work. Your work management is structured in such a way that your boss, Gwyneth, with whom you work very well, has enormous power over your promotion.

Gwyneth is an attractive 30-year-old who has supported and warmly encouraged you in your work. Recently she seems to have been around you rather more and today she has made an overt sexual approach to you. You have a range of very mixed feelings.

B4. 14 *Caretaker*

The caretaker asks to talk to you about a member of your group, Ted, who is in his forties. Ted has never been very forthcoming and is not very enthusiastic about the work, although he has been a regular attender for over a year.

The caretaker has noticed that Ted and a man who attends another class in the same building often leave together at the end of the evening. Last night he saw them embracing when they met. He is obviously much shocked and concerned for the reputation of the college and about the reactions of the other students. A dressmaking class was due to finish and could have come out at any moment! He wants you to *do* something about it.

Note: The tutor may wish to ask course members who is their 'client' at this point.

B5. RACE AND CULTURE

(For other materials covering race and culture, see also: **A1.** 19, 22, **A4.** 6, 44, **B1.** 7, **B4.** 4, 5.)

B5. 1 *Asul*
You are very unhappy in your present house. There are no other members of your community living in the neighbourhood and no prospect of a transfer since the housing authorities do not seem interested in the distinctions between your culture and that of your neighbours.

B5. 2 *Rifat*
> 'There's no point. I know I could do that job better than him. It's the same all the time. I go into the bank and they treat me as though I have no brain. The school assumes my children are having problems when I know they are very bright children. I walk into college and they try to put me on an Access course. There really isn't any point in trying to work with white people. Oh, you can't possibly know what it's like. If anyone in this place cared there would be an Asian counsellor. We're never going to be seen as normal because they're never going to give us normal jobs.'

B5. 3 *Mohammed*
Mohammed is a nurse working on a ward in which a Muslim patient has just died. He sees non-Muslim colleagues begin to move the body and rushes over. When he explains that it is against the patient's religion for non-Muslims to touch the body, they look at him as if he had just come from another planet.

B5. 4 *Sanjay*
Sanjay is very unsettled at work. He has been passed over for promotion three times and is beginning to believe he will never get on in his organisation. This does not seem to fit with the very positive feedback he gets from his managers, who have sent him on some very prestigious projects. Sanjay works long hours and seems to get little recognition for this. A comment he overheard recently, about Asians being hard workers, has set him wondering whether it is taken for granted that he will work longer hours than his white colleagues.

B5. 5 *Rehka*

Rehka is a relatively new employee. She comes to see you in some distress over the way she is treated by Vera, who has worked in the section for nearly fourteen years. Rehka feels that Vera is 'overbearing' and 'patronising', treating Rehka as though she is 'thick'. Rehka is wondering aloud whether Vera's attitude has to do with racism. Your experience is that Vera tends to come across as overbearing and patronising with everyone, including you, but her motivation, you believe, is good: she herself thinks she is being helpful.

B5. 6 *Yasser*

Yasser is very self-opinionated and dominates any group of which he is a member. He has been on the receiving end of a lot of racist treatment and on this he is particularly outspoken. He usually interrupts when women start to speak but defers to older men.

B6. DISABILITY

(For other materials covering disability, see also: **A1.** 6, 20, 25, **B1.** 2, **B7.** 4.)

B6. 1 *Jessie*
(Role Play)

You have been in your job for several years and although you have been told repeatedly that your work is excellent you have never been promoted or encouraged in your applications for other jobs. You are sure your disability has something to do with this.

B6. 2 *Carmen*
Carmen has been working for you for the past four months. She has put a lot of effort into the work, but seemed less committed over the last week or two. You say you've noticed a bit of a change and ask whether there is anything troubling her. She is silent for a minute or two and then, rather hesitantly, starts talking.

Carmen has an obvious physical disability and walks with a pronounced limp. She tells you that although she was overjoyed to start with at getting a job, she has noticed that the way people look at her and talk to her is different from the way they behave towards other people. She is very upset by this – all she wants is to be an 'ordinary' employee.

B6. 3 *Tony* (who has been referred by a teacher who works with adults with learning disabilities)

'It feels like they're laughing at me. I told them I was going to be an accountant. I'm good at maths, I know I am. But they just keep saying I'm thick. I work really hard. If you work really hard you can be anything you want to be, can't you? Why do they keep telling me I'm stupid? They say I'll never be any good and they laugh when I tell them. I have a lot of responsibility. I do a lot of work. I even take my niece to church sometimes. Why do they laugh?'

B6. 4 *Isabelle's sister*

'It's all Isabelle, Isabelle. "Isabelle doesn't moan. Isabelle is such a lovely girl." They just feel sorry for her because she can't walk. It's me who has to *do* everything. "Isabelle can't do the washing up. It's not her fault, is it?" If anyone tells me what a saint Isabelle is just one more time I'll scream. They just *expect* me to do things. If I left home they'd only notice when they found the dirty dishes.'

B6. 5 *Charlie*

Charlie is 16 and taking his GCSEs in two months. A severe hearing loss was diagnosed when he was 3 years old, which his father never really accepted, hoping all the time that it will improve. Although somewhat shy and withdrawn, Charlie has always seemed happy at school showing exceptional artistic talent. He has a place at a college on the other side of the city for September on a BTEC course and hopes to make a career in art.

Until this year his attendance at school has been good, but the teachers are now worried at the amount of time he has off. His mother, who accompanies him to school, says she fears his health is breaking down and thinks the college course will be too much for him. Charlie himself says he's a bit fed up and doesn't feel well in the mornings. Eventually he adds that he's embarrassed that his mother always comes on the bus with him but he doesn't want to tell her this because he thinks it might upset her and she's always been devoted to him. He's worried also about his father who thinks he ought to do something practical next year and go on to a YTS scheme like the other boys.

B7. STRESS, ANXIETY, DEPRESSION

(*For other materials covering stress, anxiety and depression, see also:* **A1.** 3, **A3.** 19, 44, 52, **A4.** 5, 17, 22. *For materials covering substance abuse, see:* **A3.** 12, 15, 17, **A4.** 18, 28.)

B7. 1 *Ophelia*
You are finding it impossible to sleep – things just go round and round in your head and you can't relax. You are wound up all the time and you have stopped working at school so all the teachers keep going on at you – which doesn't help. Your parents shout at each other a lot so, when you are at home, you are always waiting for the next outburst. You know it's all your fault really. If you were cleverer and more lovable people probably wouldn't shout so much – but it's upsetting to think about that, so you don't.

B7. 2 *Mrs J.*
Mrs J. is 82. She lives in a comfortable house on her own and does her shopping nearby. She likes to do her own housework and cooking to keep active and goes to church when she can. You feel that she is better provided for than most people her age. She wants your help to get a place in a home for the elderly. She gets very lonely and depressed because she has no friends or relatives close by. She finds the over-sixties clubs very noisy and they are too far away for her to travel to them easily.

B7. 3 *Salman*
You run your own business and have been working extra hard to keep the order books full, rather than make people redundant. You are going to see a counsellor because for the past six months you have been getting pains in your chest. Your GP has examined you and can find nothing wrong. He seems to be suggesting that you are fussing about nothing but you *know* it hurts.

B7. 4 *Dave* (whom you are unable to meet in the counselling room because the door is not wide enough for his wheelchair)

> 'I'm at the bottom of the pit. What kind of a life is this? I hate every minute of it. Every sodding minute. People are always telling me how life is what you make of it, smile and the world smiles with you, aren't I wonderful to keep so cheerful. One day I'll just tell them to fuck off. I'd love to see their faces. But I can't let mum know how I feel. I know she hates all the messing about with me. She never says anything but I can tell she gets so tired sometimes. I'm just a burden to everybody. I have dreams sometimes where I'm going to do a proper job and I'm going out with a really nice girl. As if any girl would want a useless cripple.'

B7. 5 *Helen*

> 'It's stupid – I know I shouldn't be feeling like this. I've got a nice place to live, enough money – well, we don't have to worry about the basics but I suppose no one's ever got enough money for all the things you want to do, especially with the kids getting older. All the things on the telly they keep showing. Of course they're going to want them. Still, they're good kids really – I shouldn't moan. And now they're at school I don't get so tired and sometimes Len takes them out so I can get on with things. I started looking for a little job a few weeks ago but Len said I wouldn't be able to cope and anyway the kids still need me at home at the minute. I suppose he's right. I wouldn't want them to suffer just because I'm feeling a bit down. I'm sorry, I know I'm wasting your time really. I shouldn't be going on like this. There must be other people with real problems you need to see.'

B7. 6 *Pearl*

Pearl is 39 and has come to the clinic because she is having menopausal symptoms (night sweats and hot flushes) since having an operation for fibroids twelve months earlier. She says she worries a lot about her health and doesn't feel she could go to her GP because she had had investigations for pains which showed nothing wrong. Her doctor might think she was a hypochondriac. Pearl is clearly very anxious and upset when talking about her symptoms. She has hardly slept for weeks since someone told her it could be the menopause.

How does she feel about starting the menopause? Pearl feels dreadful: she wanted to have another baby. They had put off having a baby in her second marriage, so that now it might be too late.... Pearl's life is full of stress. Her mother died last year; she gave up full-time work to help look after her grandparents (both in their nineties) who live nearby. Now she works part-time but does as much in half the time as she did before. Her husband has his own business and he works very hard too. They never relax together, and now her 16-year-old son from her first marriage is growing up and growing away from her...

B7. 7 *Katie*

Katie is a bright, pretty 15-year-old. She is the youngest of six children and the only one to excel at school work. She was told two years ago by her mother that she was not her father's child but she continues to be close to him and indeed says she feels he spoils her. For some time she has behaved promiscuously and six months ago she became pregnant. This caused great tension in the family. Her mother wanted her to keep the child so she could bring it up as her own but her father insisted on an abortion. Although her parents claim they disapprove of her sexual behaviour they continue to allow her to live in separate accommodation in a caravan in the garden (the reason given being that she and her sister hate each other and quarrel so much). At the weekends she works as a waitress in a local hotel, often not getting home till 1.00 a.m.

Since the abortion she has been seeing you regularly. She has become more and more withdrawn but recently she has confided that she is having an affair with a 20-year-old married man who treats her in a rough and bullying fashion, often making her very unhappy. She discusses with you how she can end this affair. Two days later her friends bring her in in a semi-conscious state saying she has swallowed a bottle of aspirin.

B7. 8 *Bill*

Bill joined your club two weeks ago. He is pale, thin and rather fragile-looking. His clothes show a tasteful concern for fashion but are rather shabby, his hair is long and carefully styled and his hands always clean with well-manicured nails. He sits at the side speaking to no one. You join him for a coffee. He says he's been in care since he was 4 – various foster homes and community schools. He reveals that he is 19, although he looks much younger, and says that when he was 18 social services ceased to be responsible and found him a bed-sitting room. He lives on social security, having had different jobs as a waiter, a shop assistant and with a hairdresser. He attends college part-time and would like to be a social worker. He feels very lonely. No one wants him. He says he doesn't trust people. He gets very depressed, and often thinks of suicide. He looks at the bottle of aspirins on the mantelpiece but he hasn't got the guts . . . one day he will have. He's interested in black magic and astrology. Sometimes he gets so mad he smashes everything in his room, then he sleeps for two days. He loves cats – he's just acquired two kittens but his landlord has complained about them.

B7. 9 *Julie*

Julie has come to the clinic about her pre-menstrual tension. She talks about feeling depressed and bloated before her period. She doesn't sleep very well, having no trouble in getting to sleep but waking up in the night and thinking and worrying for hours about all sorts of things. She says that she and her mother have gone into business together and things aren't working out too well. Their business is in rather a specialised field and it will take time to build up contacts and orders. Julie is wondering whether to take a part-time job in the meanwhile.

B7. 10 *Gurnam*

You have a free period in your teaching day, and as you are walking to the staffroom an older pupil whom you used to teach a year ago bumps into you. He is in great distress, rushes past you, kicking the wall and, you think, swearing under his breath. You follow him quietly, asking to speak to him. Eventually he stops and tells you that he has been suspended from school for threatening to hit a member of staff. You have never known Gurnam be aggressive before, and also think privately that the member of staff whom he threatened has an ability to inflame situations. In probing the situation which led up to his suspension, tears well up in his eyes, and you slowly learn that his younger sister has been taken into hospital, dangerously ill.

B7. 11 *Kuldip*

Kuldip has come to see you following an episode of anorexia which led to her being rushed to hospital, near to death. She talks in a flat tone, telling you her life story, including the fact that she was raped at 13 but told no one for fear that she would ruin her chance of marriage. She tells her story with no emotion – as if it happened to someone else.

APPENDIXES

APPENDIX 1: CATEGORISATION OF THE FORMS OF RESOURCE MATERIAL

SECTION A1	Base form	7, 9, 15, 16–23, 25–27, 29–31
	Client direct speech	1–6, 11–13, 28
	Role play	8, 10, 14
	Horseshoe role play	24
SECTION A2	Base form	1–3, 5–13, 16
	Role play	4, 14–15
	Horseshoe role play	1, 17
SECTION A3	Base form	1–25, 26–36, 38–48, 50–52
	Role play	49
	Horseshoe role play	37
SECTION A4	Base form	1–4, 6–13, 15–28, 30, 31, 33, 35, 38–48, 50–63
	Role play	14, 32, 34, 38, 49
	Horseshoe role play	5, 29, 36, 37
SECTION B1	Base form	7, 9, 13
	Client direct speech	1, 2, 4, 8
	Role play	3, 10, 12
	Linked role play	5, 6, 11
SECTION B2	Base form	1–4, 8–9, 12–16
	Client direct speech	10
	Linked role play	5–7
SECTION B3	Base form	5–8, 12–13
	Client direct speech	11, 14
	Role play	1, 3, 4
	Linked role play	2
SECTION B4	Base form	1, 3, 7, 8, 11, 14
	Client direct speech	2, 5, 9
	Role play	4, 6, 12, 13
	Horseshoe role play	10
SECTION B5	Base form	3–6
	Client direct speech	2
	Role play	1
SECTION B6	Base form	2, 5
	Client direct speech	3, 4
	Role play	1
SECTION B7	Base form	2, 6–11
	Client direct speech	4, 5
	Role play	1, 3

APPENDIX 2: EXAMPLES
OF CASE MATERIAL HANDOUTS

UNCONDITIONAL POSITIVE REGARD

Imagine the people below. Try to conjure up a picture of them in your mind's eye. Notice your own feelings and responses to each (don't analyse their situation). How much difficulty do you think you would have in really listening to the person?

0 = No problem
1 = Slight problem listening
2 = Considerable problem listening

A. Betty is a single mother who finds it difficult to cope with her three young children. She is pregnant again and has decided to have the baby in the hope that the father will decide to come and live with her.

B. Joey is in his early teens and has been thieving since before he can remember. He sees nothing wrong with this, saying, 'They get the insurance money, don't they. It doesn't hurt anyone.'

C. Baldip is very self-opinionated and dominates any group in which he is a member. He has been on the receiving end of a lot of racist treatment and on this he is particularly outspoken. He usually interrupts when women start to speak but defers to older men.

D. Violet spends a considerable proportion of the meagre family income on cigarettes and cheap wine. She says she has to have some pleasure in life. She frequently complains about not having enough money to buy nice clothes and toys for the children, bus fares, fresh fruit or vegetables and so on.

E. Dave was in the armed forces until recently. His wife died just after he came out, leaving him to manage his two children. He will not allow them to talk about their mother, saying things like 'Don't be silly, crying won't bring her back', and 'We have to look forwards, not backwards.'

F. Your colleague is working with a family where the frequent rows between the two partners is causing the children considerable distress. The partners are considering splitting up but your colleague's view is that breaking up causes more problems than it solves and that they should stay together and stick with their marriage vows.

ETHICS AND PRACTICE

Read each case study and, in your group, discuss the following:

1. How would you feel?

2. Which course(s) of action would meet your needs?

3. Which, if any, section of the BAC Code(s) applies?

A. You are Fatima's line manager. She tells you, in confidence, that a white member of your team is calling her names and making racist remarks (never in public). She is distressed and angry about this but begs you not to do anything in case the whole team 'turns against' her.

B. You are a health visitor making regular visits to a single parent who is depressed and frustrated at having a low income and no family or friends to turn to for help with the children. On this occasion he bursts into tears, telling you that he used his belt on the 5-year-old and can't forgive himself. The little one is covered with angry welts and bruises.

C. You work in a project for young people and you are Tim's key worker. Tim has a reputation for being a very 'difficult' young man and you are pleased that using your counselling skills has helped you to build up a good relationship with Tim. Central to the trust he has in you is that you have kept all his disclosures completely confidential. Today he is looking very pleased with himself and when you ask why he tells you how he has ingeniously stolen a number of items from project workers and users. You express your unhappiness about theft and he goes sullen and sulky and says if you tell anyone he'll never trust you or anyone else ever again.

D. Damien is your colleague working in adult education. The people you work with are often lacking in confidence after being labelled 'failures' at school. You feel that Damien is very patronising towards the women students, but some of them seem to enjoy his flirtatious approach. You are also inclined to be tolerant because he spends a lot of his own time 'counselling' (as he calls it) students after work. Yesterday you saw him in the town holding hands with one of the students as they walked along together, laughing and talking.

E. Lucy has a degenerative disease which is causing her increasing pain and distress. One day you are delighted to find her calm and happy. She asks whether she can tell you something in complete confidence and you say 'Yes' without really thinking. She tells you in great detail her plans to commit suicide.

COUNSELLING SKILLS IN MANAGEMENT

Read the following case materials. In your group, discuss:

a) the extent to which counselling skills would be useful in the situation;

b) the limitations of counselling skills in a managerial role.

A. You are in a meeting. You know that two of the participants dislike each other. As the meeting progresses it becomes clear that whenever one of them puts forward a suggestion, the other opposes it, almost, it seems, irrespective of the content of the suggestion. You are aware of an increasing level of discomfort in yourself and other participants.

B. You are meeting with a junior colleague to discuss her work performance. She agrees that she is not putting all her effort into work at the moment but feels sure she will be able to do enough to meet an important deadline in three weeks' time. You feel sure that she is kidding herself, knowing the amount of work involved. You have been told, in confidence, by the person who works most closely with her that her partner has just been offered and accepted a post in Japan.

C. Rehka is a relatively new employee. She comes to see you in some distress over the way she is treated by Vera, who has worked in the section for nearly fourteen years. Rehka feels that Vera is 'overbearing' and 'patronising', treating Rehka as though she is 'thick'. Rehka is wondering aloud whether Vera's attitude has to do with racism. Your experience is that Vera tends to come across as overbearing and patronising with everyone, including you, but her motivation is good: in Vera's own eyes she is trying to be helpful.

D. You are line manager to a new member of staff. He has confided to you his insecurity and uncertainty about his new role and you have used your counselling skills to show empathy and give him support. However, he has a very authoritarian manner to cover this insecurity and is generally putting people's backs up, including yours at times. You are beginning to realise that he is taking your support and understanding to mean that he does not need to change.

E. Dave's wife left him several weeks ago, taking their children with her. All his colleagues were very supportive at the time (including yourself), knowing how shocked and upset he was. However, since then he seems to have lost interest in work. He misses deadlines, is offhand with people and rumours are circulating about his drinking. His colleagues are now fed up with his behaviour and two have approached you, as his line manager, to complain (unofficially).

INDEX

abortion 157
acceptance 8, 13, 83, 89–91, 181
adaptation of material: level of training,
    according to 55–66; work context,
    according to 66–70
adolescence: generally 159–60; role play
    159; sexuality and 164–5
affective development: training, as part
    of 16–17
ageing 162
anxiety 173–7
appraisals 87
audio recording 53–4

beginnings: counselling skills used
    after different role 104–5; difficult
    previous session, after 108–9; first
    counselling session with
    self-referred person 105; generally
    103; previous experience of
    counselling, 'first' session after
    107–8; referral from another
    person/agency 106–7
behavioural development: training, as
    part of 16–17
bereavement: abortions 157; gay and
    lesbian 70, 155–6; generally 148;
    individuals and families 149–54;
    miscarriages 157; multiple ungrieved
    losses 158; role play 151, 152, 153,
    155, 156; stillbirths 157; 'unnoticed'
    155 ff
boundaries: friends, relatives, with
    133–4; generally 129; other
    professionals, with 130–2; role play
    130, 131, 132
boundary breaks: confidentiality 136–7;
    generally 135; money issues 137–8;

presents 138; sexual 139

case material: adaptation of material 55
    ff; empathy, to develop 20–2; grading
    of 20; items of information in 55;
    procedure for 22–5; purposes of
    19–20
case vignettes 19
certificate in counselling skills course:
    generally 56; use of key questions in
    58, 60, 61
challenge 99–102
change and transition: additions to
    family 160–1; adolescence 159–60;
    ageing 162; employment changes
    162; health changes 161–2; leaving
    home 159–60
client role: personal role play 27–8;
    projected role play 28
cognitive development: training, as part
    of 16–17
complexity of material: alteration of
    62–6
confidentiality 136–7
confrontation 99–102
congruence 92–4
content of course 10
context: adaptation of material
    according to 66–70
core conditions: acceptance 89–91;
    congruence 92–4; empathy 83–8
counsellor role 28–9, 36, 37
cultural differences 169–70

demonstration fishbowl role play 41,
    46–7
depression 173–7
developing the relationship 95–102

differences: accounting for 13, 70–1, 169–70
diploma in counselling or psychotherapy: generally 56–7; use of key questions in 58, 62
disabilities 171–2
discrimination 13, 70–1
doubling 41, 47, 48, 50, 53

emotional debriefing 35, 39
emotions: *see* feelings
empathy: case material for development of 20–2; case studies 84–8; challenging and 99; development of 20–2, 84–8; importance of 7–8, 83; key questions 60, 84; meaning of 7–8; reassurance distinguished 87; role play 86, 87, 88; self-awareness and 9; trainers, importance for 12
employment: changes in 162; loss of 142
empowerment 11
endings: counselling relationships 113–14; first-session 111; generally 110; more difficult counselling relationships 114–15; more difficult sessions 111–13; role play 113
equal opportunities 13, 70–1
ethics: Code of Ethics and Practice for Counselling Skills 118; Code of Ethics and Practice for Counsellors 118; Code of Ethics and Practice for Trainers 10; generally 118, 182
excuse me role play 40, 45

families: additions to 160–1
family role play: *see* group and linked role play
feedback: generally 29–31; horseshoe role play and 40, 44; observer role and 29, 36, 45, 46, 54; tutor, from 39, 40, 44
feelings: acceptance of 8; awareness of 8; expressing, importance of 6–7; separation from others' 8, 20, 59; signals indicating 8; trainees' own 8, 20; vocabulary to communicate 8
freeze frame technique 52

gay and lesbian trainees/clients 70–1
group and linked role play 41, 47–52
group process 12

health: changing patterns of 161–2
heterogenous groups: adaptation of materials for 66–7, 68
higher degrees in counselling or psychotherapy 57
homogenous groups: adaptation of materials for 66–8
horseshoe role play: acceptance, for, 91; boundaries, for 132; challenging, for 102; end of session difficulties, for 113; generally 40, 41–5; referrals, for 121, 128; sexual relationships, for 166

imagination: development of 19, 20; use of 19, 22
inexperience 120–2
Interpersonal Process Recall 54
interruptions to counselling relationship 116–17
introduction to counselling courses: generally 55–6; use of key questions in 58, 59

key questions: case material procedure and 23–4; congruence, for 92; developing relationship, for 95; empathy development, for 60, 84; projected role play procedure, in 38; purpose of 23; referrals, for 119, 122, 124, 127; use of at different levels of training 55, 58–62
knowledge: basic element of training, as 14

learning: trainees' responsibility for 10–12
leaving home 159–60
letting go 33, 35, 39
linked role play: *see* group and linked role play
listening 31–2, 33–4, 37, 38–9
loss: complexity of material and 62–6; generally 141; key questions to understand reactive processes 61; objects, of 142–3; relationships, of

144–7; role play 142, 144, 145, 146, 147

managers: counselling skills for 69–70, 183; trainees' prejudices about 132
miscarriages 157
money issues 137–8

National Vocational Qualifications 57

objectives of courses 10–11
observer role: feedback and 29, 36, 45, 46, 54; generally 29–31
one-to-one counselling 69
organisations: counselling skills in 69–70, 183

personal development: trainees' 8, 9–10, 15
personal role play: client role 27–8; development of 36; meaning of 27; procedure for 31–5
presents 138
projected role play: client role 28; meaning of 27; procedure for 36–9
projection: trainers' need to manage 9

race and culture 169–70
rationale 6–7
recordings 53–4
referrals: beginnings and 105–7; generally 119; inappropriate professional and personal relationships, as result of 122; key questions 119, 122, 124, 127; limitation of time or work overload, as result of 123; limitations of personal nature, as result of 124–5; more appropriate mode of working, to 125–6; own inexperience, as result of 120–2; receiving 127–8; role play 121, 123, 128; role using counselling skills, from 120
relationships: developing 95–102; loss of 144–7; sexual 165–6
role play: acceptance, for 91; adaptation of material 55 ff; adolescence, for 159; bereavement, for 151, 152, 153, 155, 156; boundaries, for 130, 131, 132; challenge, for 100, 102; client role

27–8; counsellor role 28–9, 36, 37; demonstration fish bowl 41, 46–7; disability, for 171; empathy, for 86, 87, 88; endings, for 113; excuse me 40, 45; group and linked 41, 47–52; horseshoe see horseshoe role play; interruptions to counselling relationship, for 116; items of information in 55; loss, for 142, 144, 145, 146, 147; observer role 29–31; personal see personal role play; preparation for through case material 20; projected see projected role play; purpose of 26; referrals, for 121, 123, 128; rondelle 41, 45–6; sexuality, for 164, 165, 166, 167; tutor observation 39; variations 40 ff
rondelle role play 41, 45–6

self-awareness: importance of 9–10
self-evaluation 11
sexual boundaries 139
sexuality: abuse of power and 167–8; discovering 164–5; generally 163; relationships and 165–6; role play 164, 165, 166, 167
sexual orientation 70–1
sexual relationships 165–6
skills development: basic element of training, as 14–15, 16; role play and 26
stakeholders 53
stillbirth 157
stress 173–7
supervision 62

trainees: personal development 8, 9–10, 15; relationship with trainers 12; responsibility for learning 10–12; self-awareness 9–10
trainers: empathy of 12; relationship with trainees 12; self-awareness 9; training for 13
training: elements of 13–17; levels of 55–7
trust 83

unconditional positive regard 8, 13, 83, 89–91, 181

video recording 53–4